IN ACCORD WITH NATURE

D1570595

In Accord with Nature:
Helping Students Form an Environmental Ethic Using Outdoor Experience and Reflection

by
Clifford E. Knapp

Clearinghouse on Rural Education and Small Schools
Charleston, West Virginia

Clearinghouse on Rural Education and Small Schools
Appalachia Educational Laboratory
P.O. Box 1348, Charleston, WV 25325
www.ael.org/eric/

Library of Congress Cataloging-in-Publication Data

Knapp, Clifford.
   In accord with nature: helping students form an environmental ethic using outdoor experience and reflection / by Clifford E. Knapp.
       p. cm.
   Includes bibliographical references and index.
   ISBN 1-880785-20-X (alk. Paper)
   1. Environmental ethics—Study and teaching. 2. Environmental ethics—Study and teaching—Activity programs. 3. Environmental sciences—Philosophy. I. Title.
GE42.K64 1999
179'.1'071–dc21   98-45539
   CIP

ERIC/CRESS and the author are grateful for the following permissions to reprint: "A Teacher's Environmental Code of Ethics" by Maureen Zarrella is reprinted with permission from the author. The dedication to *The First Book of Ethics* by Algernon D. Black is reprinted with permission from the American Ethical Union and from Jonathan Black, son of Algernon D. Black.

This publication was prepared with funding from the U. S. Department of Education, Office of Educational Research and Improvement, under Contract No. RR93002012. The opinions expressed herein do not necessarily reflect the positions or policies of the Office of Educational Research and Improvement or the Department of Education.

The ERIC Clearinghouse on Rural Education and Small Schools is operated by the Appalachia Educational Laboratory (AEL), Inc. AEL is an Affirmative Action/Equal Opportunity Employer.

∞ The paper used in this publication meets the minimum requirements of the American National Standard for Information Sciences—Permanence of Paper for Printed Library Materials, ANSI Z39.48-1984.

Contents

Foreword

Howard Kirschenbaum[1]

Thirty boys and girls, ages 11–14, and a half-dozen adults meander into a small cabin deep in the northern forest. The first arrivals flop down on the floor cushions or against the walls. One picks up a guitar and starts strumming. A few sing along, while others write in their diaries or give one another a friendly shoulder massage. They call each other by unusual names—Hat, Sunny, Unc, Squeaky, Manhattan John. The last arrivals straggle in a few minutes later, having finished their after-dinner cleanup chores. When all are present, Unc takes the guitar and everyone joins in a rousing song. The camp's nightly meeting has begun.

Twelve-year-old Hat is *brains* tonight. It's his job to run the meeting, following the routine that is by now well established. "Okay, we'll begin with validations. Who wants to start?"

A young girl begins, "I want to validate Paul Bunyan for encouraging me on the hike. Every time I felt like quitting, he urged me on or let us rest for a few minutes. Thanks, Paul."

One of the adults grins and says, "Don't mention it."

"I want to validate Squeaky," says another, "for asking me to be her partner on the 'blind walk.'"

When validations have run their course, Hat continues, "Okay, who's got an agenda item?"

An 11-year-old girl called Sis says, "*I* do."

"Topic?" asks Hat.

"It's teasing. There's too much of it going on around here."

"Okay," asks Hat, "How much time?"

"Fifteen minutes," says Sis, and Hat writes *Teasing—15* on the newsprint on the wall.

"Who else?" asks Hat. "Manhattan?"

"Right," says Manhattan John. "The raccoon is back in the garbage again and kept me up all night. Does anyone have a shotgun to lend me? No, I'm just kidding, but seriously, can't we do something about it?"

Hat writes *Raccoon* on the newsprint and asks, "How much time on the agenda do you need?"

"Seven minutes and 42 seconds," says Manhattan John, and everyone laughs.

"Squeaky?"

A 13-year-old girl speaks up, "There are some people who still haven't put away their stuff from the hike. I'm getting real tired of seeing that junk littering the Frisbee field. I wish you'd put your stuff away so those of us who want to play Frisbee can! Also, there are several candy wrappers scattered from one end of the field to the other."

She didn't sound squeaky at all. "How much time do you need?" asked Hat.

"None," said Squeaky, "I said what I had to say."

A junior high school earth science class watches their teacher write three choices on the chalkboard.

- Because it's against the rules and I could get into trouble if I got caught
- Because stealing is wrong
- Because sooner or later I'll be rewarded for doing the right thing

"Why don't you steal?" asks the teacher. "I suspect most of you are honest most of the time. Well, what keeps you honest? I've written three possible reasons on the board. I want you to rank these from most to least important. Put the main reason you don't steal first, then the next most important reason, and finally, the least influential reason you don't steal. Everyone think for yourself, write your answer in your notebook, and then we'll talk about it."

A lively discussion on the subject of values and morals follows. Everyone has ideas on why people do or don't do the right thing in life. After a while the teacher asks the class, "Does anyone have the slightest idea why we're talking about this subject in a science class?" No one does. Then the teacher writes one more word on the board, *Pollution*, and repeats the question. Gradually students begin to catch on.

"Oh yeah, polluters are doing the wrong thing."

"So how do you get them to pollute less?" the teacher asks.

The students have different ideas.

"You make rules so they get in trouble if they get caught breaking the rules."

"No, you show them how they are hurting the environment."

"No, you reward them for not polluting."

"No, why should you have to reward someone for doing the right thing. They should just do it automatically."

"Yeah, well they don't, so you have to use threats."

The teacher writes another set of choices on the board:

- Pass a law requiring industrial emissions below the level of 50 parts per million by the year 2010

- Allow industry to trade pollution credits for all emissions below those levels

- Pay industry a reward for meeting the reduction targets each year

Then the teacher says, "I want you to rank these in order from the one you think will be most effective in reducing greenhouse gases to the one that would be least effective. Justify your answer, first by giving your opinion on the best way to motivate someone to do the right thing, and second by showing me the science and math behind your answer. I want you to choose one of the following three greenhouse gases and one of its sources. Then show me how you calculate the levels of emission over the next five years using your favored plan."

Later, after the students have talked to a variety of people in the community, including some local business and industry leaders, the teacher asks, "I'd like you to think of *one thing you could do*, personally or as part of a group project, to minimize air pollution in our town. Choose something you could do because you think it's the right thing—not because you're worried you'll get caught if you don't and not because you expect to get a reward. Then we'll go around the room and give everyone a chance to say one thing you will do for the environment because you think it's right. Feel free to say 'I pass' if you'd rather not say."

⚜⚜⚜

Robert, a third grader wearing a Calvin Klein shirt, Dockers khakis, and Nike cross-trainers, looks like he's at the edge of tears. Some of his classmates look sympathetic at his plight. Others look angry for what he did.

"I just forgot," Robert explains, "I didn't mean it."

"Yeah," says one of his less sympathetic classmates, "you didn't mean it, but Gerby could have died because you forgot to feed him."

"But he didn't," justifies Robert.

"But he *could have,*" rejoins his interrogator.

The teacher intervenes, "All right now, we all make mistakes. Let's not pick on Robert about this. I'd like you all to stand up. . . . Now, everyone who *always* remembers to fulfill their responsibilities, who never forgets to do what they're supposed to, sit down. . . . Okay, look around. You're all still standing. You can sit down now and take out your notebooks. Gerby's our class pet, and we saw how he could die if we don't take care of him. What other things in this world will die or become unhealthy if we don't take care of them? . . . Okay, now that you've made your own list, let's get your ideas up on the board. Who'll be the recorder? Josh, thank you; come on up. Now we'll go around the room and each of you can say one thing on your list."

Within a few minutes, the list up front contains 15 items, including everything from *trees, my pet, South Fork* (a local river), and *the lawn* to *my baby sister.* The teacher continues, "All right, that's a great list of living things in this world that need to be taken care of. The last thing I want to ask you to do is to choose one of them that seems particularly important to you and write a sentence in your notebook that reads, 'I will help take care of _____ by doing the following: _____.' This is a little contract with yourself to take care of a part of the world that is important to you. If you are ready to commit yourself to doing this, sign your name below the sentence. Now let's have three volunteers who signed their contracts read them aloud to us."

⋆⋆⋆

If I were to ask what these three stories have in common, you might note any number of similarities. They all involve young people. They all occur in structured groups—a summer camp, a junior high school science class, a third-grade class. They all involve active and experiential learning. In each instance, one or more adults have structured the situation to give young people an opportunity to consider their effect on the world around them. In each case, there are particular issues regarding the natural world—a littered Frisbee field, industrial pollution, an endangered class pet; but there are also more universal values issues to learn about—consideration for others, doing good because it's right, and fulfilling our responsibilities to ourselves, others, and the land around us.

There is another thing these stories have in common that is not so readily discernible. Each story involves the author of this book, Clifford Knapp. I didn't invent these anecdotes. They are scenes and settings I actually observed, and in each case, Cliff Knapp was the group leader, teacher, or consultant to the program.

The first vignette was at a children's camp Cliff operated in the Adirondack Mountains of upstate New York. It was the Human Relations Youth Adventure Camp (HRYAC). I directed the institute that sponsored the camp, but Cliff conceived the idea and codirected the program for many of its 13 consecutive summers. At HRYAC, young people had responsibilities toward the group and the setting. If they didn't do their part in meal preparation or cleanup, they and their fellow campers went hungry or had dirty plates. If they left a mess around camp, as on the Frisbee field, they learned how that impacted their friends and were motivated to change. If their words or actions hurt others or contaminated the land they lived on, the issue was brought up at the nightly meeting and everyone worked on the solution and learned from it; for it's easier to see in the small community of camp how we are interconnected with the land. At HRYAC, young people learned to be accountable for their actions. As the nightly meetings demonstrated, they saw how their small deeds could make a real and positive difference in the world around them.

Encouraging each of them to take on a new camp name helped free them from old patterns of thought and behavior. And change they did. Parents mentioned it with gratitude. I saw the effect of this three-week experience on my niece and nephews and children of close friends. And, especially, the campers noted it, saying then and for years after that it was one of the most important growth experiences of their lives. I know that more than a few college admissions counselors had to read about HRYAC for the essay on "one of your most important learning experiences." When one former camper tragically died at 16, her parents scattered her ashes over the lake near HRYAC because they knew that's what their daughter would have wanted.

Picture Cliff Knapp also in the junior high school earth science class. In the early 1970s a number of approaches to values education were gaining popularity, including *moral development, values clarification, and values analysis.* Knapp was a pioneer in seeing new connections between teaching about values and teaching outdoors. His approach to teaching about the environment with a focus on values helped influence a generation of educators and youth camp leaders to go beyond teaching the facts, concepts, and skills of the subject matter, important as they are. Rather, this newer approach urged teachers and youth leaders to help young people appreciate the relationship of nature and outdoor knowledge to their own lives and values.

The earth science teacher above was integrating this approach into the curriculum. Students were learning science, but they were also learning about values and ethics. They were learning about right and wrong in general and in relationship to the environment. They were being asked to make value judgments and yet to justify these judgments with facts and numbers. This is higher-level thinking and problem solving. Students are more motivated and engaged in this type of learning. They make meaning of the subject matter, which research indicates leads to greater comprehension and retention.

It is not only the science curriculum that is filled with wonderful opportunities for teaching environmental values and ethics. Language arts, social studies, art, and other subject areas are filled with similar, rich opportunities. From this recognition, it is a short leap to realize that the informal or "hidden" curriculum of the school, including the many serendipitous events that occur throughout the school day, often provides meaningful opportunities for teaching values and environmental ethics. A good example is the third-grade teacher who seized such an opportunity when the class was giving young Robert a hard time for failing to fulfill his responsibility toward their class pet.

Cliff was typical of the many teachers he worked with as director of the outdoor education program for Ridgewood (New Jersey) Public Schools. In this role, which sadly is an increasingly rare position in schools today, Cliff was responsible for the learning program when classes attended weeklong sessions at the district's outdoor education center. Here the instructors worked with teachers to combine their subject–matter study with outdoor experiences—scientific experiments, literature readings inspired by nature, mathematical calculations using nearby objects and places, journal writing, and the like. Cliff also extended learning beyond the outdoor education center, showing teachers how to bring outdoor education back into the classroom and the community. He explained how to give whole classes or individual students assignments right outside the school or in their own homes and yards to enhance academic learning. He taught them to bring outdoor knowledge and ethics into the classroom through class projects involving the land and living things. For almost two decades, Cliff has utilized this approach with thousands of teachers at the Lorado Taft Field Campus of Northern Illinois University and, through his writing and consulting, to educators around the globe.

Today, there is a growing emphasis on teaching values, ethics, and character in schools and other youth settings. There is also a growing awareness that for such education to be successful, it must be comprehensive. Comprehensive values education involves direct teaching and instruction about right and wrong, civic values, and character traits like respect, caring, trustworthiness, and other virtues we want all children and adults to demonstrate. It also requires modeling those traits to provide young people with living and attractive examples of meaningful values to live by. And, finally, comprehensive values education gives students well-structured opportunities to learn positive values and ethics experientially—by thinking for themselves, making choices, and acting on their choices.

If we are to help young people develop an environmental ethic to live by, our approach to teaching and learning must be similarly comprehensive. Clifford Knapp offers such an approach in this volume. Based on a long and fruitful professional career on the cutting edge of outdoor and environmental education, he has synthesized a compendium of approaches for thinking about and teaching outdoor knowledge, appreciation, and ethics. It is not just a recipe book of specific activities, although there *are* many good activities described. Rather, it is a cogent presentation of many useful perspectives and approaches that can be incorporated into teaching an environmental ethic to young people. It is based on sound philosophy steeped in the tradition of Leopold, Schweitzer, Naess, Carson, and other seminal thinkers about the interconnection of the land and all its inhabitants. This is a thought-provoking and eminently practical book for teachers of all subjects and levels, private and public agency interpreters, and youth and club leaders in many settings. It is a hopeful direction for a new millennium.

Preface

Maureen Zarrella's code for teaching about the environment (see box on next page) provides a general framework and guide for teaching the what, why, how, when, and whether of making ethical choices. This code consists of some of her beliefs, attitudes, values, and principles centering on one aspect of teaching and learning. She cares deeply about protecting and maintaining life on the planet. She believes in teaching about the interdependent connections in the environment. By recognizing the importance of respect, peace, tolerance, giving back, appreciation for wonder, beauty, and joy, she has identified the bases for establishing some guiding principles for her teaching. When she ventures outdoors to teach, she and her students will also learn from the natural world. This code of ethics for teaching helps set the tone for this book. It can inspire teachers everywhere. However, inspiration is only the beginning; teachers also need to follow Maureen's example and write their own guide to the journey.

This book outlines various perspectives on environmental ethics—special ways of viewing and acting toward nature and human nature. It presents several alternative strategies for teaching environmental values lessons and suggests some structured experiences to help learners respect and care for the natural and built world. It briefly defines several types of environmental ethics, including the Wise Use movement, social ecology and justice, ecofeminism, stewardship/conservation/ecomanagement, Aldo Leopold's ecological conscience or land-as-community concept, Albert Schweitzer's reverence for life, deep ecology/bioregionalism, traditional or indigenous approaches, animal welfare/rights, and radical ecoactivism. The primary purpose of the book is to help educators—including school teachers, youth leaders, and private and public agency interpreters—plan, conduct, and assess their educational efforts to help children and youth develop a more complete and defensible environmental ethic.

This book offers some approaches for introducing values and ethics education into educational programs. The contents are especially important today because of the growing need of youth for

A Teacher's Environmental Code of Ethics

I will teach only that which is life affirming:
   the preservation, reclamation, and protection of our planet
   home.
I will teach connections:
   the myriad of ways that plants, soil, rocks, trees, animals,
   and humans are dependent on and enriched by one another.
I will teach respect for the rights of all others to a peaceful and
natural existence:
   plants, animals, people; regardless of national affiliation,
   political persuasion, economic condition, race, religion,
   or gender.
I will teach peace:
   with other people, with the flora and fauna, with the
   entire biotic organism.
I will teach tolerance of other views:
   knowing that there are many approaches to even the tall-
   est mountain, but always the universal goal.
I will teach giving back:
   time, energy, matter; by recycling, working for environmental groups and causes, using biodegradable materials, planting trees, growing prairies.
I will teach appreciation for the wonder and beauty of our
planet home:
   the shape of a cloud scudding across a summer sky; the
   autumn beauty of a phalanx of geese responding to an
   ancient call, the quiet solitude of a snowy wood at twi-
   light, the joyful and raucous riot of color that is a spring
   meadow.
I will teach the joy to be found outdoors.
I will take my students out of doors.
I will let the outdoors teach them . . . and me.

—Maureen Zarrella

direct contact with the air, soil, water, plants, and animals. Some believe that young people have been separated or alienated from the land by our modern, technological, consumer-based society. A broad, ecological view of the land was first proposed by Leopold, one of the most influential ecologists, writers, philosophers, teachers, and re-source managers of this century. As we approach the next century, humans face a rapidly growing world population, critical food short-ages, and shrinking green space. To complicate matters, many of the planet's inhabitants are severely polluting the sources of their life-support system, taking resources at unsustainable rates, consuming more and more manufactured products, and using up more than their fair share of Earth's riches. As a result, the distance between the world's haves and have-nots is widening, and the land is slowly being degraded. Despite these realities, this book does not take a "gloom-and-doom" approach to change. In contrast, it takes a "can-and-should-do" approach.

Ethics, a branch of philosophy, deals with making the right choices for the right reasons. It is the study of standards of right-and-wrong conduct, duty, and judgment. It involves deciding what human ac-tions will do the least harm to others. Choosing the right and good ways to act toward others is moral decision making. Developing an environmental ethic includes making sacrifices and limiting per-sonal freedoms to benefit the larger community. It requires people to ask not only why, what, how, when, and where to do a thing, but whether a thing should be done at all. A personal code of ethics provides a framework for decision making as we design our lives.

Ethical choices are usually difficult because many of life's chal-lenges are complex and people disagree on the best ways to live. H. L. Mencken wrote, "Every complex problem has a simple, obvious solution that is wrong." It follows then that if you try to simplify complex ethical questions, you are likely to come up with the wrong answers.

Behaving morally requires listening to your conscience and con-sidering the well-being of community members who will be affected by what you do. Thus, moral behavior relates to our duties and obligations toward others or our consideration of their rights. How you define *community* is very important. Until this century most philosophers included only human members in their definition. Deciding what was right or good dealt with how human behavior affected other people, not the other-than-human world. Of course, if you expand your definition of *community* to include other animals such as bees or bears, and plants such as trees or thistles, your decisions become more difficult. Continuing to expand your idea of the community to include water, air, rocks, and soil increases problems even more. When you expand your idea of community still further to include whole natural systems such as forests, prairies, rivers, and oceans, you have created a difficult personal dilemma. Imagine the enormous problems if you considered the well-being of all of the planet's inhabitants as community members and tried to behave accordingly. Many people believe we need to think on this broad global scale, but how can we really accomplish this?

Environmental ethics is an applied field of study dealing with this expanded community concept. It "guides human experience of and relations with the natural world in pursuit of sustenance and well-being."[2] Advocates for environmental ethics place great value on the natural environment. Most people who are concerned with environmental ethics care about and respect things like wilderness; endangered plants and animals; vanishing old-growth forests; clean, free-flowing rivers and streams; food free of toxic chemicals; pure air; healthy prairie ecosystems; and much more. They realize that sometimes they must give priority to the welfare and survival of nonhuman organisms or whole natural systems. However, this does not mean that they always give low priority to what humans want or need. They believe that humans and other inhabitants of natural systems are all interconnected; when we harm the natural world, we ultimately harm ourselves.

People from various perspectives—including philosophy, ecology, social sciences, land management, and education—participate in the ongoing conversation about environmental ethics. For example, philosophers interested in environmental ethics have asked questions that require a broad perspective:

Should we be more concerned with the survival of individual plants and animals or with whole populations of them?

Do plants, animals, rocks, or ecosystems have certain moral rights that people should recognize or do people simply have certain duties, obligations, and responsibilities to protect them?

Are the living conditions on Earth seriously threatened by human activities to the point where we must change our belief and value systems?

What is the place of people in nature? What is our role in protecting it now and for future generations?

Are nonhuman organisms just as important as humans, and if so, do they have intrinsic or inherent worth apart from our use of them?

These questions cause us to wonder what is good for people in the short run and what is best for people *and* the nonhuman world in the long run. If we consider more than just our immediate needs and desires and extend our view of community beyond humans, we can make more thoughtful decisions about the rest of the Earth. This book attempts to show how to arrive at better answers to these and other sorts of questions.

Society often calls upon the science of ecology to probe questions about the interrelationships of living things within their environment. Ecologists wrestle with a more concrete set of questions:

Are certain plants or animals rare or overpopulated in an area?

What happens when a plant or animal from another continent is introduced into an ecosystem?

What are the effects of certain toxic chemicals on the reproduction rates of a plant or animal?

Are there any biological controls for getting rid of certain unwanted plants or animals?

How does the thinning ozone layer affect the life cycle of frogs and other amphibians?

How do plant and animal population numbers change in an area over a period of time?

How rapidly does a particular plant or animal extend its range in an ecosystem?

What are some effects of different air pollutants on specific organisms and climates?

Making ethical choices about the environment also involves asking social scientists for answers to social, economic, and political questions. Social scientists ask questions such as these:

Can we learn important ideas for living in today's world from indigenous or traditional people who live close to the land?

Is there a relationship between how we treat certain groups of people and how we treat the Earth?

Can we continue to develop land for human uses and develop new technologies in attempting to improve our standard of living?

What are the costs and benefits of building a dam on a river?

How much should industry pay for the convenience of polluting land or waterways?

What are the human costs of locating a dump near economically deprived people?

Who should absorb the costs of transporting and storing nuclear waste?

How should a community be zoned to allow for various types of development?

To what extent should a candidate consider short-term economic gains in a party's positions on environmental issues?

These are questions whose answers can guide us in our search for ways to make the world a better place for all life. But there are more questions, on a very practical level, that land managers ask:

When should hunting and fishing seasons begin and end for different animal species?

What are the characteristics (e.g., age, sex, size) of the animals allowed to be taken by hunters, fishers, and trappers?

How fast should power boats be allowed to travel through waters occupied by manatees?

How many people should be allowed to visit a certain park in a given season?

What is the best way to prevent certain undesirable plant and animal species (e.g., purple loosestrife or zebra mussels) from spreading?

What is the best way to deal with large populations of deer in a particular area?

How close to certain species of nesting birds should bird watchers be allowed to observe?

Which woodland fires should be fought and which should be allowed to burn until they go out naturally?

These examples give us an idea of the complexity of the questions and variety of issues addressed daily by scholars, scientists, and regulators. At the broadest level, environmental philosophers ask questions that probe whether human actions are right, good, and valuable. They also ask what parts of the world ought to be given moral consideration. Philosophers ask questions about the proper role of humans as they conduct their lives. Philosophers who ask questions about environmental ethics talk about obligations, rights, duties, social justice, and virtue.[3] They use logical and critical thinking as tools for uncovering new knowledge.

Natural scientists usually pose questions and test hypotheses through controlled experiments and descriptive studies in the physical world. Their goal is to gather information (data) and discover relationships among different factors (variables) at work in the world, but they do not always know what they will find. As they apply scientific methods to probe their questions, new questions often arise. Often, they do not know how society will use the new knowledge gained from their studies. They are supposed to be as objective as possible by trying to ignore or minimize their personal feelings when seeking out answers.

Social scientists take much the same approach in the social world as natural scientists do in the physical world. They engage in careful analyses of social structures, economics, and politics. In modern communities around the world, social scientists are asked to apply their expertise in informing decision makers, who use their knowledge to decide how to organize and conduct governments.

In short, scientists are called upon to answer questions about what *is*, while philosophers are asked to help address questions about what *ought to be*.

In reality, land managers administer peoples' *uses* of land and water more than they manage the land itself. They are guided by principles of ecology as well as social, economic, political, and legal processes. For instance, if a large percentage of their budget is derived from the sales of hunting and fishing licenses or sporting equipment, their decisions may be influenced by the concerns of individuals who hunt, fish, or engage in outdoor activities. If administrators of these land management agencies are appointed by a certain political group, their decisions may be affected by the party line. On the other hand, if state and federal laws dictate specific actions governing the use of land, managers are usually compelled to follow those dictates. In this case, ethical choices come into play only insofar as they influence the formation of regulations or laws.

How can the answers to questions raised by these various groups guide us in our search for ways to make the world a better place for all life? Some say they cannot; others say they can. What do you think?

Educators interested in environmental ethics and values have many difficult questions to answer, too. They must address not only all the questions previously raised but a host of others related to teaching and learning:

How should we deal with controversial land issues in the curriculum?

When are we justified in imposing our own viewpoints on our students, and when should we let them decide what is right for themselves?

Should we try to change student values about the environment in a particular direction? If so, toward which values?

If we try to influence their values in certain directions, what are the best methods to do that?

Should students get involved in community action projects even if some people in the community disagree?

If they do, which projects are appropriate for certain grade levels and which are not?

Does teaching about certain land problems and controversies create fear or apathy in some students?

What environmental concepts, skills, attitudes, and values are the right ones to study at different age levels?

This book deals with some of the basic ideas underlying these questions asked by philosophers, scientists, land managers, and educators. It attempts to help teachers and youth leaders make sense out of teaching about environmental ethics. It focuses upon blending theory and practice. A few words of caution are appropriate: the field of environmental ethics is extensive, and philosophers do not agree on answers to many questions. Donald VanDeVeer and Christine Pierce describe environmental ethics as a jungle. David Mathew Zuefle puts it this way: "It's a daunting and impossible task to attempt to reduce a good deal of ethical philosophy and volumes of topically-specific thinking into a few paragraphs of nontechnical language. . . ."[4]

This complexity is also true for the fields of education, science, and land management. This book can only help readers begin the process of exploring these areas. Karen J. Warren suggests another metaphor for viewing the depth of these fields:

> When one describes a lake by looking down at it from above, or by only skimming across its surface, one gets a limited and partial view of the nature of the lake. It is only when one dives deep and looks at the lake from the bottom up that one sees the diversity and richness of the various life forms and processes that constitute the lake.[5]

This book attempts to take a brief swim in several lakes, but does not dive too deeply. For those wanting to explore beneath the surface, the references at the end provide several opportunities. This book does not offer a complete program or curriculum, but suggests a variety of swimming strokes and floatation devices for reaching the main goal of helping students arrive at the distant shore—developing an environmental ethic. There is no one best way to help students do this, but this book attempts to point you in the right direction by asking some of the right questions.

Although I respect diverse opinions about philosophy, science, land management, and the art and science of teaching and learning, this book is not value free. I believe that if our present, highly consumptive and materialistic North American lifestyles are not simplified, the quality of life will diminish and our survival on the planet will be threatened. Also, I believe that once people understand more about the environment and how it works, they will want to change their beliefs, attitudes, values, and behaviors to live more gently on the Earth. I believe that certain outdoor experiences conducted by schools and other organized groups are essential for today's youth as they develop and refine their environmental ethic. This book is designed to guide leaders through these complex topics. Let's begin this journey.

—Clifford E. Knapp

Notes

[1] Dr. Kirschenbaum is Frontier Professor of School, Family and Community Relations in the Warner Graduate School of Education and Human Development at the University of Rochester. He is the author of 22 books, many of which deal with values education, including *100 Ways to Enhance Values and Morality in Schools and Youth Settings.*

[2] Tony Baltic, "Technology and the Evolution of Land Ethics," in *Nature and the Human Spirit: Toward an Expanded Land Management Ethic*, ed. B. L. Driver, Daniel Dustin, Tony Baltic, Gary Elsner, and George Peterson (State College, PA: Venture Publishing, 1996), 265.

[3] Timothy Beatley, *Ethical Land Use: Principles of Policy and Planning* (Baltimore: Johns Hopkins University Press, 1994), 13.

[4] Donald VanDeVeer and Christine Pierce, eds., *People, Penguins, and Plastic Trees: Basic Issue in Environmental Ethics* (Belmont, CA: Wadsworth, 1986), x; David Mathew Zuefle, "Animal Rights Versus Environmental Ethics," *Legacy* 7 (March/April 1996): 32.

[5] Karen J. Warren, "Feminism and Ecology: Making Connections," *Environmental Ethics* 9 (1987): 20.

Acknowledgments

This book is dedicated to my parents, Louise and Ed Knapp. Among other things, they gave me the gift of life, a childhood filled with opportunities to explore nature, and the foundation for my environmental ethic. Although raised in suburban New Jersey, I enjoyed many outdoor adventures in the undeveloped spaces of my community as a child. Box turtles wandered into our yard from nearby woods, minnows swam in the brook that ran through town, reeds temporarily shielded us from signs of civilization, soil banks gave us opportunities to dig forts, and rock cliffs invited us to climb. I can remember seeing the orioles' basket-shaped nest reappear each year in the elm across the street. The turtles, minnows, reeds, soil banks, elm, and nest have long since disappeared. Only the rock cliffs remain. In my mind's eye I can still see the path curving through the patch of woods across the street and the skunk cabbage growing in a low, wet place there. A neighbor's house now stands where the path curved and the skunk cabbage grew. I can recall fishing for minnows in the pond fed by our brook. A shopping mall occupies that pond site now, and nothing swims there. In our back-yard, where I raised earthworms, a storage shed now stands. Worms can't live there anymore. My mother, the family storyteller, still laughs when she describes the catfish I caught nearby and released in our bathtub. She confirmed this fact on the phone, and I won a bet with a disbelieving friend who called her to verify my story. I wonder if any catfish are caught today in that brook or are swimming in a bathtub somewhere in town?

These are some of the childhood experiences that shaped my beliefs, attitudes, and values about nature and laid the foundation for a broader environmental ethic. As I reflect fondly on those early years, I wonder: Are these simply the nostalgic recollections of a bygone time and place or do these memories carry a modern-day message or moral imperative for us? Rachel Carson raised similar questions in her book, *The Sense of Wonder:*

> What is the value of preserving and strengthening this sense of awe and wonder, this recognition of something beyond the boundaries of human existence? Is the exploration of the natu-

ral world just a pleasant way to pass the golden hours of child-hood or is there something deeper?[1]

My deeper responses to these questions lie within this book. I am grateful to my parents for helping me gain the experiences and knowledge that produced my present-day ethic. Yes, there have been others who helped shape my thoughts and feelings about nature, but none have been more influential than my parents. They allowed me the freedom to explore my town's wild spaces and to learn to love and respect the land.

I also thank Milton McClaren of Simon Fraser University in British Columbia. He went beyond my expectations in critiquing the first draft of this manuscript. He helped me to grow as he raised key questions, expanded awareness of my hidden biases, referred me to further readings, pointed out some contradictions and inconsistencies in the text, and generally lifted my thinking to a higher level. Nevertheless, I must accept full responsibility for the final selection of the contents.

Another influential person in my life has been my son, Ryan. Of all the people I've known, he modeled a simple lifestyle and inspired and taught me more about walking gently on the earth. We will miss him and his shining example as a dedicated environmentalist.

Once again, Jan Woodhouse and Pat Hammer served as able, eagle-eyed editors who, with the able assistance of Stan Bumgardner, helped polish the final text. This book is clearly an example of cooperating to reach a goal.

Notes

[1] Rachel Carson, *The Sense of Wonder* (New York: Harper & Row, 1956), 88.

What Is Environmental Ethics?

The land is always stalking people. The land makes people live right. The land looks after us. The land looks after people.
— Annie Peaches (Apache),
The Spell of the Sensuous

Where It All Began

Tracing the early evolution of humanity's intimate connection and care of the land—what is now known as environmental ethics—is a task too big for this volume. This chapter provides only a thumbnail sketch of the origins of environmental ethics. There are many excellent books to help the reader understand the field. Roderick Nash provides a historical overview in his book *The Rights of Nature: A History of Environmental Ethics.* In the prologue, he offers a simplified view of how ethics may have developed. He suggests early humans learned to shift their concerns for right and good behavior beyond their own self-interests to include their families and tribal units. Then as various tribes banded together, social ethics slowly spread to regions and whole nations. By grouping together, societies increased their chances for survival. Later, races felt the bonds of connection to all of humanity and to the inhabitants of the land. Nash acknowledges that most people have not fully achieved this ideal state of fair and just treatment for everyone. Some humans still attack and kill their own kind, but many ideas of right and wrong behavior are embodied in the laws and rules of conduct that protect and sustain communities. Even these societal rules are altered under certain conditions, allowing for the execution of murderers and the waging of war.

As societies became more complex and urbanized, their close ties to the land weakened. Only during the latter half of the twentieth century have some people tried to recapture the land ethic derived from their indigenous roots and to extend moral consideration to some animals and plants. Western society has a long way to go in adopting our ancestors' close connections to the Earth's other-than-human inhabitants. However, many societies here and around the world have a long history of intimate connections to nonhuman nature that still persists today.

In the nineteenth century, a few isolated voices in the United States advocated for wildlife, forests, scenic places, and moral consideration for nature. Henry David Thoreau moved to Walden Pond in 1845 to live simply, commune with nature, and write about humanity's Earth connections in his journals. In 1867 John Muir encouraged respect for "the rights of all the rest of creation."[1] John Wesley Powell published *The Exploration of the Colorado River* in 1875 and recorded his impressions of nature's beauty.[2] During this same period (from 1860 to 1900), the Conservation movement was born, representing a new awareness and concern for nature. During the past century in the United States, more and more individuals have realized the need for preserving wild nature for its own sake, even though others think society has gone too far in that direction.

According to Eugene C. Hargrove, environmental ethics as a professional field emerged with the first Earth Day celebration in April 1970.[3] Environmental activists began asking philosophers about the ethical issues underlying environmental policies. In 1979 a new journal, *Environmental Ethics*, helped to establish an appropriate label for the field and encourage authors to debate how humans should interact ethically with nature.

The Meaning of Environmental Ethics

Environmental ethics, explains Nash, embodies two ideas: "First, some people believe that it is right to protect and wrong to abuse

---

The Perils of Teaching Ethics

This book is dedicated to a great teacher who was killed in the year 399 B.C. by the people of the ancient city of Athens.

Why did they kill him?
They killed him for a crime.
What was the crime?
He was accused of corrupting the young people of the city.
How did he do that?
He asked questions.
Why would that hurt anybody?
By his questions he made them think.
What's wrong with that?
He made them think about things they believed.
How could that do any harm?
When people ask questions and think about things they believe, they may not believe the same after that.
And the people of Athens killed him for doing that?
Yes, they did.
Why did he do it?
Because he loved truth and he wanted to find truth.
Who was this teacher?
He was a stonecutter. He earned his living by cutting marble for the buildings and statues of the city. But in his free time he was a teacher.
What was his name?
His name was Socrates.
What subject did he teach?
His subject was ETHICS.

—Algernon D. Black, *The First Book of Ethics*

---

nature (or certain of its components) from the stand-point of human interest." A second and more complex interpretation "is that nature has intrinsic value [apart from how humans view it] and consequently possesses at least the right to exist." Nash elaborates that "human beings are the moral agents who have the responsibility to articulate and defend the rights of the other occupants of the planet. Such a conception of rights means that humans have duties or obligations toward nature. Environmental ethics involves people extending ethics to the environment by exercise of self-restraint."[4]

Various authors have offered a variety of definitions of environmental ethics.

From Joseph R. DesJardins:
Environmental ethics assumes that human behavior toward the natural world can be and is governed by moral norms. A theory of environmental ethics then must go on to (1) explain what these norms are, (2) explain to whom or to what humans have responsibilities, and (3) show how these responsibilities are justified.[5]

From Kristin Schrader-Frechette:
Environmental ethics is a combination of both disciplines [ethics and ecology]. [It] aims at enhancing our relationships both with others and with the world around us.[6]

From Paul W. Taylor:
Environmental Ethics is concerned with the moral relations that hold between humans and the natural world. The ethical principles governing those relations determine our duties, obligations, and responsibilities with regard to the Earth's natural environment and all the animals and plants that inhabit it.[7]

From Karen J. Warren:
"Environmental ethics" is the name for a variety of positions which consider the non-human natural environment and human relationships to it as morally considerable.[8]

From Donald VanDeVeer and Christine Pierce:
Reasonably addressing two issues constitutes the benchmark of any plausible environmental ethic: "What sorts of things have moral standing?" and "What are acceptable principles" . . . to help decide what are permissible (or obligatory) trade-offs in the cases in which the lives or welfare of some things that

possess moral standing conflict with the lives or welfare of other entities possessing moral standing?[9]

Each of these five definitions provides a way to think about environmental ethics. A main purpose of this book is to help you, and eventually your students, clarify your own thoughts on what it means to have an environmental ethic.

David Mathew Zuefle sees the concept of environmental ethics used in at least two ways in the literature. First, it refers to the *application of any ethical theory* related to humanity's treatment of nature. Second, it refers more restrictively to a *particular human moral approach to nature* involving whole ecosystems.[10]

This book examines a broad range of ethical theories related to how humans treat nature. No particular approach to relating to nature is promoted over others, although the reader may detect some of this author's range of worldview preferences.

To summarize, the applied field of environmental ethics is a branch of philosophy that questions how humans relate to nature more than how humans relate to other humans. By seeking answers to these questions, we investigate our moral conduct both as individuals and as communities. This form of inquiry views the planet as made up of interconnected human and nonhuman elements, processes, and systems and asks how all elements can live together in harmony. Behaving responsibly toward the Earth, some environmental ethicists believe, requires us to make sacrifices so all living things can exist under healthy and sustainable conditions. Such changes necessitate thinking about who we are in relation to others and developing systems of beliefs, attitudes, values, and principles to guide us as we live compatibly with the rest of Earth's inhabitants.

Worldviews: Biocentric and Anthropocentric Ways of Seeing the World

People's culture includes the shared or common meanings they attach to different events and what they believe to be true. According to VanDeVeer and Pierce, "What we are doing and what we collectively *will do* depends in large part on what we *believe*—about the way things are, will be, or can be—and (importantly) what is good, what is right, or what it is permissible to do."[11] The ways in which

5

people relate to their environment and perceive their lives is called a *worldview*. Jack Levin and James L. Spates list some questions, the answers to which can serve as indicators of a worldview:

What is our perception of time? Are we oriented toward the past, present, or future?

How do we relate to the physical world? Do we emphasize mastery over, harmony with, or subjugation to the environment?

How do we view the nature of activity? Are we motivated by becoming more spiritual or by doing or achieving things?

What is the nature of human relationships? Are they hierarchical, collective, or individualistic?

What is human nature? Is it good, bad, or neutral?[12]

These are some of the questions to ask when you examine your own worldview. The answers to these questions can have implications for how individuals interact with the world.

In fact, the ways people relate to time, the physical world, daily activities, relationships, and their beliefs about human nature are essential components of a worldview. In the field of environmental ethics, two contrasting worldviews describe the extremes on a continuum. These are "biocentric" or life (Earth) centered and "anthropocentric" or man (human) centered ways of seeing the world.

When people strongly value nature and give it moral consideration, their worldview is closer to the biocentric end of the continuum. They usually believe that nature has value in and of itself, and possesses rights, or that humans have obligations, responsibilities, or duties to protect it. G. Tyler Miller, Jr. calls this worldview "sustainable-Earth society ethics."[13]

[This worldview is] based on the beliefs that humans are part of nature and that our primary purpose is to share the Earth's finite resources, care for all people and nonhuman species, interfere with nonhuman species only to satisfy vital human needs, and work with—not against—nature.[14]

When people strongly value human goals at the expense of non-human nature, their worldview is closer to the anthropocentric end of the continuum. People in this camp believe that only the needs and wants of human beings are important when deciding what is good and right to do. Nature, according to this worldview, has only instrumental or utilitarian value; that is, its value lies in its usefulness in satisfying society's wants and needs. Nature has value for making life more convenient and comfortable or for achieving other human-centered goals. Miller calls this worldview "throwaway society ethics."[15]

> [People with this worldview] assume that human beings are apart from and above nature and that their role is to conquer and subdue nature to further human goals. Matter and energy resources are assumed to be unlimited because of human ingenuity, and endlessly rising production and consumption of material goods is considered to be the primary goal of the culturesphere.[16]

The opposite end of the continuum is critical of human domination over other Earth inhabitants. Elizabeth Dodson Gray, an ecofeminist, describes the Earth-centered worldview as an ethic of *attunement.* Attunement is an ethic of interconnectedness and relationship. She believes our challenge is to be open to ourselves, to listen and look, and to pay attention to the land despite not fully understanding how the world works. She agrees with the poet Thich Nhat Hanh: "What we most need to do is to hear within ourselves the sounds of the Earth crying." If we "hear the Earth crying," we will usually respond with concern and caring.[17]

Gray describes a human-centered ethic as based on a hierarchical worldview in which humans are on top and animals, plants, and the rest of nature are below them. She believes this illusion forms the basis of Western science and technology. She calls this an atomized ethic of self-interest. People with this worldview may not be able to "hear the Earth crying," and if they do, they may not know how to respond.[18]

In the novel *Ishmael,* Daniel Quinn, too, contrasts ways people have lived on the Earth throughout history. He calls these two worldviews *civilized* (represented in his story by the Takers) and *primitive* (represented by the Leavers).[19] The story of the Leavers began two or three million years ago and continues today in isolated places. The story of the Takers began only about ten or twelve thousand years ago with the birth of agriculture in the Near East.

Quinn believes that the Leavers' and the Takers' stories were based on two very different and contradictory worldviews. The Takers' main premise was "the world is a human life-support system, a machine designed to produce and sustain human life." It logically follows that humans were meant to rule the world.[20] The problem with this premise is that by attempting to gain mastery of the world, humans have despoiled it. The indicators of civilization (urbanization, technology, literacy, mathematics, and science) are associated with dying ecosystems. The Takers basically do four things differently than the rest of the community of living things:

1. Exterminate their competitors

2. Systematically destroy their competitors' food to make room for their own

3. Deny their competitors access to food

4. Store certain foods for periods of time (such as grains and meats)[21]

The Leavers have always searched for the answer to the question: "Is there a way to achieve settlement that is in accord with the law that we've been following from the beginning of time?"[22] The law they followed, perhaps without knowing it, has three parts:

1. No one species shall make the life of the world its own.

2. The world was not made for any one species.

3. Mankind was not needed to bring order to the world.[23]

Leavers are conscious of having a tradition, dating back to early times, passed down through their stories. That is why it is important, they believe, to preserve these traditional stories and learn from their wisdom.

Quinn's book involves an imaginary conversation between a wise gorilla teacher and a man who wants to learn how to save the world. It illustrates the two extremes of the human-centered and Earth-centered continuum. The book presents many environmental dilemmas in lively story form and provides thought-provoking metaphors to help us think through problems facing society.

Because this continuum does not exist in reality (it is a mental construct or idea in our minds), people do not function at either extreme. In fact, they may shift along this moral line depending upon the situation. For example, people who believe large mammals such as wolves or bison have a right to coexist with us might be called biocentric if they vote for the animals' preservation in the wild. In a different situation, those same people might be called anthropocentric if they vote to exterminate rats and starlings in the community because of danger to their health.

In general, anthropocentric worldviews give human wants and desires first priority and do not value nature for itself. The dualism of anthropocentric and biocentric worldviews is not really as simple as it may appear. In some cases, a decision that favors human survival also favors the survival of the rest of nature. Therefore, the ethics of people who seem to demonstrate strong preferences for nature should be studied on the basis of their underlying reasons for doing something, as well as for what they actually do. It can be difficult to identify an anthropocentric or biocentric worldview based on isolated behavior. It is much easier to identify worldviews if we ask about the motives behind people's actions and examine their lifestyles.

Chapter three will scrutinize more closely how a person's beliefs, attitudes, values, and principles interact to form the basic building blocks of an environmental ethic. When we make daily decisions and solve life problems as individuals and community members, we knowingly affect the environment. Making the best choices about how to conduct our lives demands using accurate information to inform our beliefs, attitudes, values, and principles. A person should sort out the many variables in each situation to think critically about an environmental issue.

Understanding the field of environmental ethics entails exploring the meanings of ecology, nature, technology, and human communities. These topics are all interconnected; and our views toward each can directly influence our ethic.

Notes

¹ Roderick F. Nash, *The Rights of Nature: A History of Environmental Ethics* (Madison: University of Wisconsin Press, 1989), 6.

² Benjamin Kline, *First Along the River: A Brief History of the United States Environmental Movement* (San Francisco: Acada Books, 1997), 49.

³ Eugene C. Hargrove, ed., *The Animal Rights, Environmental Ethics Debate: The Environmental Perspective* (Albany: State University of New York Press, 1992), xi.

⁴ Nash, *Rights of Nature*, 9, 10.

⁵ Joseph R. DesJardins, *Environmental Ethics: An Introduction to Environmental Philosophy* (Belmont, CA: Wadsworth, 1993), 13.

⁶ K. S. Shrader-Frechette, *Environmental Ethics* (Pacific Grove, CA: The Boxwood Press, 1981), xi.

⁷ Paul W. Taylor, *Respect for Nature: A Theory of Environmental Ethics* (Princeton, NJ: Princeton University Press, 1986), 3.

⁸ Karen J. Warren, "Warren's Proposed Model for Thinking and Writing about Environmental Issues, Ethics, and Actions" (paper presented at Macalester College, St. Paul, MN, 20 January 1993), 11.

⁹ VanDeVeer and Pierce, *People, Penguins, and Plastic Trees*, 16. The general introduction to this book provides a good summary of environmental ethics, 1-17.

¹⁰ David Mathew Zuefle, "Animal Rights Versus Environmental Ethics," *Legacy* 7 (March/April 1996): 32.

¹¹ VanDeVeer and Pierce, *People, Penguins, and Plastic Trees*, 1-2.

¹² Karen D. Harvey, Lisa D. Harjo, and Jane K. Jackson, *Teaching about Native Americans* (Washington, DC: National Council for the Social Studies, 1990), 25.

¹³ G. Tyler Miller, Jr., *Living in the Environment: An Introduction to Environmental Science*, 5th ed. (Belmont, CA: Wadsworth, 1988), 592.

¹⁴ Ibid., 601.

¹⁵ Ibid., 591.

¹⁶ Ibid., 600.

¹⁷ Elizabeth Dodson Gray, "Come Inside the Circle of Creation: An Ethic of Attunement," in *Ethics and Environmental Policy: Theory Meets Practice*, ed. Frederick Ferre and Peter Hartel (Athens: University of Georgia Press, 1994), 26-28.

¹⁸ Ibid., 25.

¹⁹ Daniel Quinn, *Ishmael: A Novel* (New York: Bantam/Turner Books, 1992), 39.

²⁰ Ibid., 69, 72.

²¹ Ibid., 126-28.

²² Ibid., 119.

²³ Ibid., 145-46.

How Do Ecology, Nature, Technology, and Community Relate to Environmental Ethics?

What people do about their ecology depends on what they think about themselves in relation to things around them.

—Lynn White, Jr.,
"The Historical Roots of Our Ecologic Crisis"

Exploring Ecology

Ecology is a branch of science dealing with the study of organisms and their relationships to their surroundings. In 1866 Ernst Haeckel, a German scientist, observed that all things were connected in nature and resembled a household. He coined the term *oekologie*, derived from the Greek term *oikos* meaning house or *household*.[1] Just before the turn of the twentieth century, *oekologie* was changed to *ecology*.

How does ecology relate to environmental ethics? Some would argue that before we make decisions about land, we must know how nature works from the scientific standpoint. Others would say that a scientific discipline like ecology is only indirectly related to such decisions because, in reality, social issues and problems are at the heart of such matters. These folks argue that science gives us only partial information about what is or might be in the universe, offering no guidance about what is right or good to do.

It is true that some environmental ethics scholars know quite a bit about ecology, while others know very little. On the other hand, some ecologists who have conducted a great deal of research outdoors have developed feelings for nature that go beyond the realm of pure science. Edward O. Wilson, for example, after almost a lifetime studying ecology, recognized three truths he had learned. The first two deal with the concepts of biological evolution and the diversity of life. The third is that "philosophy and religion make little sense without taking into account these first two conceptions." Perhaps because some scientists know something about how the world works, they have developed a deep sense of awe and respect for it. They also realize that despite what they think they know, they really do not know very much. Wilson recognized that the "Earth, in the dazzling variety of its life, is still a little-known planet."[2]

This understanding of the limits of scientific knowledge can prevent unintended problems caused by, for example, land management practices that introduce predator insects. Many scientists recognize that introducing exotic species into an area to eat other insects considered harmful to crops could lead to serious consequences for the whole ecological community. Biologist Walter Courtenay refers to such practices as a game of "ecological roulette" with few benefits and many damaging impacts.[3]

One danger that exists when making ethical choices is that scientific knowledge is used as the sole basis for deciding what should be done. This decision-making method may prove to be wrong and result in ecological damage because scientists may not understand the ecosystem or may lack sufficient information about how the world works. It is important to remember that knowing what *is* in the natural world does not necessarily tell us what we *ought* to do. This *is* and *ought* idea, called the *naturalistic fallacy*, has been debated by philosophers for hundreds of years. This debate applies when we try to use ecological concepts and principles to answer philosophical and management questions.

Exploring Nature and Environment

When we try to pick out anything by itself, we find it hitched to everything else in the universe.
—John Muir, My First Summer In the Sierra

One touch of nature makes the whole world kin.
—William Shakespeare, Troilus and Cressida

The word *nature* comes from the Latin *nasci* or *natus* meaning *to give birth*. Perhaps this root suggests that nature describes the world as it was at its birth before humans began to populate and change it. How does the original source of the word influence how we interpret the word *nature* today? This question leads to another, often-debated question: Are humans a part of nature or separate from it?

The word *environment* comes from European linguistic roots, *environuen* or *environner*, meaning *around* or *in a circle*. Perhaps the root suggests that environment is everything around us or encircling us. The same question asked about nature can be asked about the environment: Are humans a part of the environment or separate from it? The terms *nature* and *environment* are often used interchangeably in this book and elsewhere.

In *Essence I*, a set of community investigations developed by the American Geological Institute, an activity card invites students to "go out and find positive evidence that something natural happened." The card lists several dictionary definitions of the word *natural*.[4] This activity also notes: "What you see as natural may not agree with a natural scientist's view."[5]

What is nature? This question has provoked many discussions, much confusion, and thousands of pages of writing over the years. The answer does not come easily. Bill McKibben thinks the modern mind generally divides the world into two separate things: nature and human society. He defines nature as "that world entirely independent of us which was here before we arrived and which encircled and supported our human society."[6]

Neil Evernden examines two different ideas of nature:

"Nature" with a lower case "n" refers to the "great mass of otherness" on the planet (actual) and "Nature" with an upper

13

case "N" refers to a mental model (cultural) which arose in the West several centuries ago.[7]

Evernden believes the meaning of Nature (the system or model) was derived from ancient stories of Earth-based cultures and its contents were established through historical evolution. From the viewpoint of Western society, Nature once included everything. As time passed, the meaning was restricted to include everything except God. Finally, it came to mean everything except God and humans. As the meaning of nature changed through time, modern cultures developed the dualism—all is either nature or not nature.[8]

Yet, he points out, while one meaning of nature separates it from human influence, another meaning points to *human nature* or the natural element existing in people. Considering these ideas, there are at least two kinds of nature: nonhuman and human. Evernden writes, "The term *nature . . .* is a strange one, one that almost seems to invite misunderstandings." Rachel Kaplan and Stephen Kaplan also stress the confusion existing around the word: "It is clear that . . . the language for discussing [nature] is neither rich nor precise."[9]

This ambiguity does not exist everywhere. While some cultures have created the idea of nature by restricting its meaning to things outside themselves, a word for nature does not exist in some other languages because people are not aware of it as something separate from themselves.

Evernden describes two views of Nature. According to the first, *nature-as-object*, nature is believed to be governed by systems that operate by laws. Humans seek to understand how this kind of nature works so they can be better Earth caretakers.[10] In the second view, *nature-as-self*, humans are a part of nature, too, and by harming nature, they harm themselves. Both groups want to care for nature efficiently and assume that nature is a thing outside themselves that needs our help.

It appears most people in modern industrial societies view nature primarily from the nature-as-object perspective. By contrast, people in traditional societies, who tend to live close to the land, view their world more from the nature-as-self perspective. Considering that modern societies have contaminated much of the Earth, readers might consider their own responses to two questions: Which of these two societies—the industrial or the traditional—is more livable or sustainable? Which perception of nature most effectively helps us cultivate values to develop an environmental ethic that supports long-term survival of humankind?

Holmes Rolston III classified 12 types of instrumental values people see in wildlands or nature:

1. market value (using nature to give humans material comforts);

2. life support value (using biological and physical systems such as air flow, water circulation, sunshine, and nitrogen-fixation to nurture us and other living organisms);

3. recreational value (using nature for activities such as fishing or skiing or contemplating or observing scenery or wildlife);

4. scientific value (using nature as a laboratory for gaining knowledge about ecosystems);

5. genetic diversity value (using nature as a source of genetic food stocks);

6. aesthetic value (using nature's forms and patterns to please the educated eye);

7. cultural symbolization value (using nature as cultural metaphors such as the bald eagle to symbolize national strength);

8. historical value (using nature for teaching future generations about how humans lived and what existed in the past);

9. character building value (using nature as a place to take calculated risks, care for one's self, and develop qualities such as courage, self esteem, and leadership competence);

10. therapeutic value (using nature to nurture psychosomatic needs and to gain balance and psychological growth);

11. religious value (using nature as sacred and cathedral-like places to stimulate spiritual thoughts and feelings);

12. intrinsic natural value (viewing nature as having a right to continued existence for itself and not for value to humans).[11]

Because humans view nature as having these different values, the meaning of the word often varies depending upon how we benefit from it.

Through a different kind of analysis, I identified nine different images or perceptions of nature by categorizing a collection of 67 nature quotations. In these passages, writers portrayed nature as something to control for good or evil, wisdom, healer and source of joy, creative force, separate from humans, human, connected to all life, feminine, or teacher.

Rolston's typology describes what modern people find valuable about nature, while my typology portrays different sorts of relationships we can choose. Both reveal that humans are describing a variety of things when they use the word *nature*. To understand people better, listeners should ask: What do you mean by nature? Our perceptions of nature are important influences in the formation of our environmental ethic.[12]

The popular media have sometimes represented nature as something to be feared. Newspapers often refer to natural disasters and destructive natural forces such as volcanic eruptions, wildfires, floods, hurricanes, and tornadoes. Films have used natural themes to excite and scare viewers. Consider movies such as *Jaws, Anaconda, Arachniphobia, Twister, Volcano, Godzilla, King Kong, Gargantua, Deep Impact*, and many others. These examples depict nature as violent and something to be feared.

In the early 1980s, the United Nations (UN) Environment Program proposed a *World Charter for Nature*, containing five general principles:

1. Nature shall be respected and its essential processes shall not be impaired.

2. The genetic viability of the earth shall not be compromised. . . .

3. Special protection shall be given to unique areas, to representative samples of all the different types of ecosystems and to the habitats of rare or endangered species.

4. Ecosystems and organisms . . . shall be managed to achieve and maintain optimum sustainable productivity, but not in such a way as to endanger the integrity of those other ecosystems or species with which they coexist.

5. Nature shall be secured against degradation caused by warfare or other hostile activities.[13]

Let us examine the first principle. It leaves several unanswered questions: What is the meaning of *nature* in this principle? How is respect to be shown? How is impairment to be assessed? How much impairment is too much? The UN General Assembly adopted the *World Charter for Nature* in 1982, but the United States did not sign the document.[14] Our UN representatives may not have been ready to sign at that time because of a belief that preservation of nature would require us to sacrifice economic growth, which is a cornerstone of our market economy.

Anthropologists Willett Kempton, James Boster, and Jennifer Hartley studied how the American people view environmental problems and humanity's interaction with nature. As part of a study of environmental values, they conducted semistructured interviews with 46 people. Twenty were chosen from the general public; the remainder were selected from a range of specialist groups—grassroots environmentalists, coal industry workers, congressional staff working on environmental legislation, and automotive engineers. The researchers wanted to interview people holding a wide range of worldviews. Three cultural models of nature were identified:

1. Nature is a limited resource upon which humans rely.

2. Nature is balanced and interdependent, resulting in unpredictable "chain reactions" that affect species.

3. The market devalues nature and leads to our failure to appreciate it and to the idealization of the environmentalism of indigenous peoples.[15]

The first model reflects a human-centered idea that people depend upon limited resources for their survival. It can include the concept that our wastes enter natural cycles and eventually return to us. For those holding this model, one reason to protect nature is out of concern for human health, both physical and psychological. They view nature as their home and believe polluting it damages their living areas. These people are strongly motivated to protect nature to assure their own survival.[16]

The second cultural model relates to human interactions within nature. The researchers consider these ideas as among the most important in their research and identify three interrelated subconcepts. First, different parts of nature (e.g., species) are so interdependent that changing one can affect others through a series of chain reactions. Second, these interdependencies are so complex the interactions are impossible to predict accurately in advance. Lastly, because of this reality, humans should not interfere with nature.

Even though these ideas relate to the field of ecology, a wide variety of people have applied them more broadly to other situations. The significance of this model is that it leads some Americans to be conservative about changing nature, even if the separate components seem unimportant to us. The model does not define which components are relevant or how large a change will cause the chain reactions. Kempton, Boster, and Hartley conclude these two cultural models differ somewhat from scientists' models of ecology. Most scientists would modify this model to a certain extent, but the simplified model still holds up in general.[17]

The third cultural model of nature reflects a three-part set of beliefs. First, modern economic and social systems devalue nature; second, a lack of contact with nature leads to a lack of concern for nature; and finally, nonindustrial peoples are thought to place value on the environment.

Several informants in the study believed the American capitalistic society fosters excessive consumption and displays of wealth at the exclusion of more important values. They stated nature is devalued because of the difficulty in assigning a market price to it. These Americans concluded that our economic system is at odds with environmental protection and that we need to reduce consumption levels in the future.[18]

Some informants attributed a lack of environmental concern by some of the American public to infrequent contact with nature. They believed this distancing leads to a lack of respect and a diminished concern for environmental issues. When the researchers compared this cultural belief to other sociological findings, they found only a few studies that investigated the relationship between outdoor contact and environmental concern. Some of these studies identified a statistically significant relationship, but none determined which came first, environmentalist values or a positive outdoor experience.[19]

The beliefs that nature is devalued by society and that most members are alienated from nature lead to comparisons of modern society with earlier periods in our history. A few informants mentioned Native American cultures and other cultures with small-scale economies as models of environmental sensitivity and minimal impact. According to the researchers' findings, about three-quarters of the public accept this belief. The fact that people often quote the land-use message attributed to Chief Seattle may indicate the source of this belief. As anthropologists, the researchers agree that many societies with simple technology and low population density live in long-term sustainable balance with nature. They also cite two examples of indigenous peoples who eventually had negative impacts on nature over a 500-1,100 year span. They suggest the cultures encouraging sustainable resource use are the ones that have survived intact and remain visible today. They question whether these societies consciously created their proenvironmental practices, beliefs, and social structures. The researchers conclude that societies that have not established long-term sustainable use of nature "must eventually either change their uses of the environment or destroy themselves."[20]

These cultural models of interrelationships in nature and humanity's relation to nature are important because they form the basis for American society's concept of environmentalism.[21] Kempton, Boster, and Hartley determined from their study that a total of 46 statements in the fixed-form survey met their criteria for deciding what most (two-thirds or more) of the American public agree upon. Consensus items that reveal beliefs relevant to developing an environmental ethic included these statements:

- People have a right to clean air and clean water.
- We have a moral duty to leave the earth in as good or better shape than we found it.
- Our obligation to preserve nature isn't just a responsibility to other people but to the environment itself.
- Because God created the natural world, it is wrong to abuse it.
- Nature may be resilient, but it can only absorb so much damage.

- We should return to more traditional values and a less materialistic way of life to help the environment.[22]

If these consensus items accurately reflect the ideas of most Americans, attempts to teach environmental ethics in schools will be wel-
comed.

In contrast, a recent survey of college freshmen revealed dwin-
dling interest in social issues and in becoming involved in cleaning
up the environment. *The Economist* reported a survey by the American Council on Education of 350,000 students in 665 colleges and
universities. The percentage of students intending to participate in
environmental cleanup programs fell from 34 percent in 1992 to 19
percent in 1997. Since the first annual survey in 1966, today's students registered more political detachment than ever before. Sev-
enty-five percent considered financial success to be essential or very
important; in comparison, only 41 percent placed importance on
seeking a meaningful philosophy of life. This finding represents a
complete reversal of the attitudes and values reported by students in
the late 1960s. Obviously, it is difficult to assess the environmental
beliefs, attitudes, and values of an entire nation. Since many educational decisions are made on the local level, it may be more useful to
assess these indicators in the community. Knowing how the majority
of the dominant groups in town think and feel is essential before
implementing plans for teaching about environmental ethics.[23]

David Orr, a professor of environmental studies, suggests that to
achieve ecological literacy, people must learn how to have a dialogue
with nature. He cites Wendell Berry's questions as a way of guiding
the form, structure, and purpose of this conversation: "What is here?
What will nature permit here? What will nature help us do here?"[24]

Our understanding of the term *nature* is very important in shaping how we teach about environmental ethics. If we are able to view
nature as a vital part of ourselves, we are more likely to behave in
ways that will perpetuate the Earth's systems. An environmental
ethic serves to guide us in reaching that goal.

Exploring Technology

*Technologies can help us work together, communicate, net-
work, solve problems internationally, and understand com-*

plex systems. They can also mystify, alienate, and isolate. I
guess there is a need for a technological ethic as well as an
environmental one.

—Milton McClaren, letter to author

Our technologies are the products of our ingenuity—the means for solving the problems we encounter in living. Our value choices about technologies impact our worldview in several ways.

While modern technologies provide many benefits, some harm the world's ecosystems. A growing number of critics believe most schools do not engage students in the research and critical thinking needed to debate intelligently the issue of appropriate and inappropriate technologies. In developing an environmental ethic, we need to determine what issues students need to consider about the place of technologies in the Earth's ecosystems.

Technology, like food, is a part of human existence. We need both. As Neil Postman explains, we should not be against food, but it makes a lot of sense to select a proper diet carefully and to eat the right amounts. Technology education should aim "at students' learning about what technology helps us to do and what it hinders us from doing."[25]

Tony Baltic defines technology as the means to provide for human sustenance and well-being. A narrow view of the term conceives of technology as meaning hardware, objects, or physical transformations such as cups, pencils, computers, videos, and many other tools. An expanded view includes systems of thought and ways of gaining, organizing, and utilizing knowledge: alphabets, number systems, sign language, Braille, and even social organizations. The broader definition of technology has many applications to modern information dissemination in schools. Baltic believes that several inseparable connections exist among an environmental ethic, human purpose, experiences in the natural world, and technology. These components form a circular system, or feedback loop, of causes and effects. For example, an environmental ethic helps shape and guide human purpose and experiences. The natural world, in turn, shapes and guides the development of our environmental ethic.[26]

One family of educational technologies (e.g., Internet, CD-ROM, videotape) has been promoted as useful tools for teaching and learning in the information age. However, everyone does not agree, and students can become involved in interesting debates about the pros and cons of these technologies. Here is Clifford Stoll's critical view of technology: "Elementary and high schools are being sold down the networked river. To keep up with the educational fad, school boards spend way too much on technical gimmicks that teachers don't want and students don't need."[27]

Do you consider Stoll's view controversial? How would you support or refute his points? Do you believe Alvin Tofler's familiar claim that high tech results in high touch or intimate social relations? Stoll, author of *Silicon Snake Oil*, is a critic of some of the new information technologies, even though he describes himself as an astronomer and computer jock. Speaking from experience in a technological world, he writes:

> [Computer networks] . . . isolate us from one another and cheapen the meaning of actual experience. . . .
>
> During that week you spent on line, you could have planted a tomato garden, volunteered at a hospital, spoken with your child's teacher, and taught the kid down the block how to shag fly balls. . . .
>
> Computers force us into creating with our minds and prevent us from making things with our hands. They dull the skills we use in everyday life.[28]

If reading these quotations generates thoughts of agreement or disagreement or feelings of satisfaction or resentment, you may want to begin the process of critically thinking about technology. This process needs to continue with youth in schools, camps, and other learning institutions. Young people need to engage in more verbal and written discussions about the role of modern technologies in our culture. This task is similar to the blind Asian Indians examining an elephant from their different perspectives. However, technologies are more numerous and complex than a single elephant. Because this challenge is great, you may wish to begin with only three questions:

Do you believe modern computer-based information technologies

1. separate or alienate people from direct experience with nature

and the community, or manifest humanity's natural abilities to solve problems and communicate?

2. directly and indirectly pollute the environment and disrupt ecological systems, or provide ways for humans to learn more about how the world works and to restore ecosystems to health?

3. lead to inadequate and biased curricula and knowledge bases for developing an environmental ethic in students, or contribute to generating vivid examples of how humanity has lost sight of what is really important?

By limiting the analysis to these points, we are obviously ignoring many other technology issues that affect individuals and societies.

There may be several reasons why many educational programs lack or minimize serious debate about modern technologies:

1. There are many complex and interrelated science, technology, and society dilemmas that are difficult to isolate and manage conceptually.

2. Consumer-based industrial societies and their institutions are controlled by powerful interests that depend upon maintaining the status quo.

3. Educators and the public in general have not been adequately informed about the dangers of continued uncontrolled technological development and adoption.

Educators who aim to assist their students in developing an environmental ethic will need to examine the effects of modern instructional technologies on students and the environment. They should be hesitant about unquestioningly accepting the use of computer-aided instruction as an inevitable sign of "progress." In the 1940s, Aldo Leopold expressed a fear that "education . . . is learning to see one thing by going blind to another."[29]

In the early 1970s, when the field of environmental education emerged, the topic of technology was promoted as one of the key issues to investigate. For example, the *U.S. Environmental Education Act of 1970*, Public Law 91-516, encouraged the study of humankind's relationship with its natural and human-made surroundings, examining such issues as population, pollution, resource allocation and depletion, conservation, transportation, technology, and urban and rural planning.[30]

Originally, one of the goals of environmental education was to develop an ethic to counter what some saw as the rapid degradation of the planet. Bill Stapp's classic 1969 definition of the field aimed at producing a citizenry motivated to work toward solutions to environmental problems.[31] The newsletter *Clearing: Environmental Education in the Pacific Northwest* still includes creating an "environmentally literate" citizenry (ethic as product) as one aim of environmental education.[32]

Twenty years after the original legislation, the *National Environmental Education Act of 1990*, Public Law 101-619, was signed. The new law contained no mention of technology as an environmental problem, and environmental *problems* became environmental *challenges*. A new recommendation stated environmental education programs "should not advocate a particular solution to an environmental challenge."[33] The political climate has changed since 1970, but one aspect of the mission of environmental education has remained—to protect the environment. This mission apparently contradicts the U.S. Environmental Protection Agency's (EPA) statement about not advocating a particular viewpoint or course of action.[34]

Where are the curriculum materials to help teachers deal with the technologies dilemma? At this writing, there are few available. Edgar Jenkins, writing in *Connect*, the United Nations Educational, Scientific, and Cultural Organization's (UNESCO) newsletter, recognizes that "any curriculum necessarily selects, and thereby privileges certain kinds of activities and forms of knowledge and sends explicit and implicit messages about them to students and teachers alike." If educators are not familiar with *Silicon Snake Oil* or other books like it, they may not have the tools to challenge and examine more closely the veracity of claims about education technology put forward by those in power. For example, President Clinton and Vice President Gore have publicly promoted Internet usage in a memo to all federal departments and agencies, urging them to determine the added resources needed to "enrich the Internet as a tool for teaching and learning."[35]

At the same time, Gore recognizes an important point in the

technology debate: "The more we rely on technology to mediate our relationship to nature, the more we encounter the same trade-off: we have more power to process what we need from nature more conveniently for more people, but the sense of awe and reverence is often left behind." Secretary of Education Richard Riley believes "computers and other telecommunications are a vital part of a sound educational future."[36]

To maintain a balanced view of these issues, teachers need to be familiar with the arguments of technocritics such as David Orr, Theodore Roszak, Jerry Mander, Neil Postman, C. A. Bowers, Paul Wachtel, David Strong, and Gregory A. Smith.[37] If these names and their views on technology are obscure, it follows that teachers would hesitate to initiate debates about appropriate and inappropriate technologies and their effects on environmental quality. To illustrate the type of helpful information teachers need, the following facts and opinions are summarized from the *Rockford Register Star*. How might they relate to a quality existence for humans and the natural world?

- About 4.25 million people are "heavy" Internet users (20 or more hours a week).

- In 1996 the average person watched an average of 4.4 hours of television and listened to 2.9 hours of radio and .75 hours of recorded music each day.

- Office paper use today is five times what it was 20 years ago.

- Rapid gains in manufacturing productivity (the amount of output per hour of work—3.9 percent in 1996) were significantly determined by the influence of rapid improvements in technology.

- The federal government is prepared to spend up to $100 billion over five years to put a computer in every American classroom, but there is simply no proof that computers alone will make students smarter.

- In 64 of its restaurants, McDonald's is testing new computer-run robot technology that serves food in 42 seconds.

- The possibility exists that a disparity of personal computer ownership among Whites, Asians, Blacks, and Hispanics could become so large that the latter groups could be left behind.

- Of the 29 EPA Superfund cleanup sites in the United States, 80 percent of them have been created by high-tech industries.[38]

If this information stimulates further research leading to constructive debates, students and teachers will be better able to clarify their positions on various technologies.

In a special section devoted to technology in *The Wall Street Journal*, university professors Seymour Papert and Theodore Roszak debated whether computers are the saviors of education. Both made valid points to support their positions.

Roszak, the technocritic, speculated, "Would we ask John Muir or St. Francis to stroke a computer key board or stare at simulations of nature?" Roszak answered with a firm "no." He also criticized "ecology programs that seek to simulate on screen what would be better done by a real flower in a pot."[39]

Many people agree that computer technology should not be used as a substitute for multisensory experiences in nature. Virtual field trips cannot possibly impact the human brain in the same way as unmediated experiences with heat or cold, physical elation or exhaustion, and dryness or wetness. Roszak labels the World Wide Web as "the brainchild of an entrepreneurial worldview . . . shaped by commercial values."[40] People with their ethics grounded in a human-centered worldview will find it difficult to criticize technologies that support and enhance their lifestyles.

Papert, a supporter of technology, countered that his position represented the majority of information that pervades the media. *The Wall Street Journal* editors are to be commended for printing a debate on the use of technology in education. Few fair treatments of technology viewed as a social issue are readily accessible to educators or to the public.

One notable exception is a book by W. J. Rohwedder and Andy Alm, *Using Computers in Environmental Education: Interactive Multimedia and On-Line Learning.* They call for "a comprehensive, critical, and yet visionary analysis of the link between [environmental education] and education technology" and point to "problems and promises" engendered by the use of computers. Problems include technological misapplication, inequity of access, environmental activity substitution, and environmental impact. In a brief analogy, "How to Make Compu-Stew," the authors highlight some of the negative impacts of computers on the environment: air pollution, wasted paper, waste disposal, electrical energy consumption, and toxic chemicals from batteries and from manufacturing processes.[41]

There is strong support from the federal and state education agencies to use computer-based and other technologies in the instructional programs of schools. Some teachers may find it difficult to resist the use of environmentally harmful technologies when they are being pressured to do so. However, if the quality of the environment and the quality of education are both considered carefully, there may be instances when the best choice is not to use computer-based technologies. To help a teacher decide, ask yourself the following questions before deciding how to reach an objective:

Can my students learn something just as well or better without technology (e.g., using direct contact with an object on the school grounds rather than using a CD-ROM or video)?

Does some outdoor learning take longer, needing experience over a period of time (e.g., watching a flower bloom or the behavior of a bird by direct observation rather than watching a time-lapse video of the process)?

Has the use of computer-based technologies dominated instruction over the past week or month and will the use of direct, unmediated teaching methods provide a better balance for the students (e.g., using out-of-classroom and socially involving lessons rather than seat-based and noninteractive ones)?

If the answer to any of these questions is yes, the teacher should consider not using a computer-based instructional method.

Another useful resource is Susan Staniforth's *The Technology Trap, Module 1 Transportation: Who's in the Driver's Seat*. This is one of a series of publications dealing with appropriate technologies. The series' goals include critically examining everyday technologies, identifying how they shape society, exploring alternative technologies, introducing examples of appropriate technology, and enabling students to take informed action concerning the use of technologies. Staniforth believes "we all have a responsibility to ask critical and appropriate questions, examine assumptions made by technology developers, and make informed choices about the technologies we use every day."[42]

The main arguments for examining the pros and cons of information technology use in education can be summarized as follows:

1. Teaching students how to develop an environmental ethic is imperative in preserving and improving the Earth's ecosystems.

2. Technology education has become an essential component of most schools' curricula; teachers should learn how to examine critically and debate its use, in addition to learning the requisite skills to use it.

3. Current information technology education is given extensive promotional and financial priority in schools and may be limited in some places to the inculcation of the values of technology marketers.

4. Modern computer-based instructional technologies are often substituted for direct nature experiences. They tend to separate students from the natural world and impede their development of an environmental ethic.

5. The manufacture, use, and disposal of computer-aided information technologies can pollute the Earth and disrupt and contaminate natural systems.

6. The use of modern technologies in schools can contribute to the redefinition of knowledge and an imbalance of curricula in ways detrimental to the well-being of today's youth.

Therefore, more public debate should be encouraged by business, industry, and government dealing with the positive and negative influences of computers and other telecommunications-based technologies on the quality of human life and the Earth's ecosystems.

In his book *Technopoly*, Postman captures similar thoughts: "We are currently surrounded by throngs of zealous Theuths, one-eyed prophets who see only what new technologies can do and are incapable of imagining what they will *undo*."[43] If there is an environmental crisis, it revolves around a metaphorical question: How can we change the flow of a raging technological river before we drown ourselves and other inhabitants on the Earth?

Exploring Human Communities

There is no such thing as the good community. There are many good communities. . . . There is simply no way to demonstrate that one viewpoint is more valid or more moral than another. It is perhaps for this reason that social scientists have avoided the pursuit of definitions of the good community.

—Roland L. Warren, *Perspectives on the American Community*

Even though decisions about the right and good uses of nature and technology affect other people on the planet, the development of an environmental ethic that translates into improved ecosystems usually occurs in the context of communities. Whether or not we can precisely define a good community, most of us can recall belonging to special groups in our lives. We have felt emotionally committed and connected to other people for various periods of time. We may have found these supportive communities through our families or extended families, schools, places of worship or employment, or neighborhoods. Collective actions based on a sound environmental ethic can be a powerful force in creating sustainable ecosystems.

M. Scott Peck defines a community as a "group of people that has learned to transcend its individual differences."[44] Many educators think effective learning communities can be consciously designed and formed in schools. They believe that people, once committed to establishing and maintaining unity, can reach the goals they set for themselves; that individuals will agree to cooperate when they recognize that everyone is strengthened and that goals can be more easily achieved when individuals work together.

Promoting a sense of community in schools and other organizations is an important challenge for educators. Before students can lead effectively, they must believe in the value of community and learn how communities are formed and maintained. The best way to

29

determine standards for a good community is by experiencing effective groups and reflecting on how they work.

According to Joel Westheimer and Joseph Kahne, "Researchers have found that teacher behavior . . . often reflects the emphasis on individualism and autonomy so pervasive in our culture."[45] These self-oriented attitudes do not contribute much to the formation of productive communities. To overcome attitudinal barriers to community building, teachers need to develop cooperative behavioral norms and increase their knowledge and skills in community building.

Theorists have outlined various principles, ingredients, or characteristics of the community-building process. John W. Gardner lists 10 ingredients:

1. wholeness incorporating diversity;

2. a reasonable base of shared values;

3. caring, trust, and teamwork;

4. effective internal communication;

5. participation;

6. affirmation;

7. links beyond the community;

8. development of young people to carry on the idea;

9. a forward view;

10. institutional arrangements for community maintenance.[46]

Cheryl Charles lists 18 characteristics:

1. sense of shared purpose,

2. agreement on core values,

3. participation,

4. communication,

5. commitment,

6. conscious choice,

7. shared responsibility,

8. equity,

9. openness,

10. respect for differences,

11. acceptance,

12. trust,

13. collaboration,

14. reciprocity,

15. accountability,

16. efficacy,

17. perceived skill,

18. cohesion.[47]

These lists emphasize that communities are complex and that people describe their components differently. Success in building communities depends partly on individual attitudes, skills, and concepts as well as how the group members interact over time.

One sociological theory of community building developed by Ferdinand Tönnies, a German sociologist, consists of two main ideas.[48] He uses the German words *gemeinschaft* and *gesellschaft* to describe each one. These terms are metaphors for two kinds of community life lying at opposite ends of a continuum. "Gemeinschaft translates to 'community' and gesellschaft translates to 'society'." As human cultures changed subsistence methods from hunting and gathering to agriculture, and then later to modern industry, their values shifted from gemeinschaft (sacred communities) toward gesellschaft (secular societies).

According to Tönnies, gemeinschaft exists in three forms: kinship, place, and mind. The kinship form created a sense of community among families and extended families; the place form emerged from sharing a common habitat (e.g., school, neighborhood, town, or country); and the mind form was grounded in the sharing of common values, goals, and visions. To these three forms of community, Sergiovanni credits Robert N. Bellah and his colleagues with adding a fourth form—a gradually evolving community of memory, which connects people to those who came before and to those who

31

will live on past the current generation. Tönnies believed that as modern society advanced, community life shifted from gemeinschaft toward gesellschaft. For example, as community values were replaced by contractual ones, society became less sacred and more secular and impersonal. As a result, connections among people became more contrived and formal.[49]

Because these terms represent two extremes along a community-building continuum, we can use them to generalize about the nature of different communities. In reality, specific communities are composed of both gemeinschaft and gesellschaft characteristics. Both play important roles in creating good communities. According to the theory, "as gesellschaft strengthens, gemeinschaft weakens. As gemeinschaft weakens, we experience a loss of community with all of its negative consequences."[50] Sergiovanni recommends that schools move from being formal and technically rational organizations toward being communities that bond people together by kinship, place, mind, and memory. Building good learning communities requires paying attention to certain values and ways of being together.

Recently, some writers have highlighted the importance of a sense of place in the lives of people.[51] When members of a learning community study the place in which they live through direct experiences, they not only learn to love and respect it more, they establish a basis for growing closer to one another. When this occurs, students become more aware of issues and problems in their community and can take collective actions to address them by making ethical choices. The learning community then becomes the microcosm in which democratic decision making develops knowledge and skills for operating on larger regional, national, and global scales.

What does a good community with a strong sense of place look like? Roland L. Warren raises several questions related to defining a good community:

To what extent should people in the group interact on a personal and intimate basis with one another?

How autonomous should a group be when faced with competing pressures from outside groups?

How much energy should a group expend to confront their problems effectively through local action?

How should the power be distributed among the group members?

Should the community members actively participate in all of the important decisions?

How important should commitments to the group be compared to commitments to larger outside groups?

How much diversity can be tolerated within the group and still have the members feel a sense of unity?

How much conflict can exist in the group and still have it function effectively?[52]

Good communities stay intact and function without destroying the surrounding life-support systems. Environmental ethics operating in good communities consider how nature and technologies interact and how each is to be used in appropriate ways. These use issues become even more critical when people join several different communities.

The late Harvard professor Lawrence Kohlberg experimented with what he called the just-community approach in the mid-1970s. Much of his work was done at the Cluster School, an alternative high school in Cambridge, Massachusetts. His main purpose was to promote individual development by building a group-based moral atmosphere among teachers and students. "Democratic governance stands at the heart of the just-community approach. For students and teachers to overcome their reliance on traditional authority patterns, they have to learn to share democratically the responsibility for decision making."[53]

Kohlberg believed that the predominant authority patterns in most schools may be effective in managing students, but they do not fit with his theory of moral development. He believed that passive acceptance or negative rejection of authoritarian rules did not help students develop morally. He advised that students should become involved in the rule-making process so they can better understand why rules exist and why they should be followed. Students outside the decision-making process are less likely to feel morally bound to uphold rules. Logically, this principle would also apply to developing and following an environmental ethic.

The Cluster School was conducted as a direct, participatory democracy. Students met once a week for a two-hour community meeting to decide on solutions to school-related issues. Even though the larger school rules were in effect, the students had the right to interpret and enforce them in their own ways. The meetings were conducted within certain guidelines to assure success.[54]

Running a school or any other organization in this way involves a set of cooperative skills that some youth leaders do not value very much. Some of the difficulties of shifting from teacher-centered to student-centered worldviews may explain why most schools still operate by authoritarian or gesellschaft means. It is hard and tiring work to be responsible for self-government, but it is extremely rewarding when a fully functioning community is created. Kohlberg considered this a *just* approach to school business because it was democratic and the students could exercise the highest level of moral reasoning available among them.[55]

His theory suggests community life plays an essential role in moral education. A community context enables students to deal with common moral issues that are more real to them than contrived hypothetical ones. Moral judgment and individual and group action are linked closely together. Community decision making enables moral principles to come alive and take on meaning. According to Kohlberg, there are many benefits to this approach. It shows the importance of group decisions as well as individual ones. It fosters group discipline through respect for rules and cultivates values of sharing responsibility. It also demonstrates the importance of living within the necessary restrictions placed on the school by the larger society.[56] The just community is an example of moving closer to the gemeinschaft end of Tönnies's continuum. It also shows how implementing this approach creates difficulties as well as benefits. The lifelong challenges of assuming social responsibilities and practicing democratic principles are essential in developing individual and community environmental ethics.

Peck's book *The Different Drum: Community-Making and Peace* explores cooperation, communication, community-building, group dynamics, spirituality, and world peace. Drawing from his own experiences in communities, Peck identifies several essential characteristics. He realizes communities must be *inclusive* and human differences should be celebrated. Group members should commit to *coexistence* and strive for *consensus* in decision making. They should *speak out* for what they believe and, at the same time, *listen* to what others are saying. Group members should also strive to develop a *climate of safety.* Conflicts, when they arise, should be resolved *without physical or emotional violence.*

Peck advocates intentionally designing good communities, following four steps. Groups usually begin with *pseudocommunity*, a false acceptance of others involving role playing and the wearing of masks. Groups take time and effort to form, so starting this way is expected. In pseudocommunities, conflict is usually avoided rather than dealt with directly. The next step is usually *chaos*. This centers on well-intentioned attempts to heal or convert one another to a particular way of thinking. Most groups need the chaos stage of struggle and confusion to move beyond it. This step is marked by advice-giving, arguing, and adhering to one's own views. At this often painful stage, few problems are solved, and little sense of a good community is felt. The third step is *emptiness*. Preconceived notions about members of the group can prevent people from really hearing each other. Emptiness is a way of escaping chaos and making the transition to community. This stage involves emptying personal barriers to communication such as negative feelings, false assumptions, or unaccepting behaviors. It is a way of escaping chaos and making the transition to *community*, the final step. Our need to control, heal, convert, or manipulate others can be a barrier to achieving a good community. At this *final* stage, the group can begin to work on projects such as improving the environment for humans and nonhumans. If careful attention is not paid to maintaining the community over time, it may revert to earlier stages.

Peck offers some bold and practical answers to the question of how to build a good community. He recognizes that cooperating with others becomes more challenging as we move from small groups to larger institutions and organizations.

What are some ways progress toward development of a caring community can be blocked? One barrier is attitudes of exclusion or exclusiveness. For example, if people do not want to be part of a group, no one can force them to join. On the other hand, if group members do not want to include new people, outsiders will remain

35

separated. Attitudes of exclusion include these sorts of beliefs:

- It's always someone else's fault, never mine.
- It's always my fault, never anyone else's.
- I don't trust you or the others in the group.
- People are basically undependable and won't work together.
- I can do it alone. I don't need others.
- If people don't share my views, they are my enemies or don't know very much.
- I'm better than the people around me.
- I'm not good enough to be a part of this group.
- Coming together as a community will never work.
- I'm not going to let this group know who I really am.

Changing these mind-sets is never easy when you have lived with them for years. Admitting that your own attitudes may be the problem, rather than something in someone else, can be difficult. However, changing personal attitudes among group members can be the best way to change the direction of a group. One important attitude is the desire to build and maintain a group structure that supports a common vision. Here are some other personal attitudes that can contribute to the success of a community group:

- I believe in the value of people and their abilities to resolve conflicts peacefully when they arise.
- I want to be recognized for my inner goodness and accomplishments if the praise is genuine.
- I need others to function effectively sometimes and I value your support.
- Your trust for me can grow when I earn it by respecting you.
- When I am open and truthful with you about who I really am, you will respect me more.
- It is worthwhile to limit some of my freedoms sometimes for the good of the whole group.
- I can disagree with some of your beliefs, attitudes, and values and still accept you as a valuable person.

- If I try to see the world from your perspective and really listen to you, I will understand you better.

- Knowing that we share some common values will help us celebrate our differences.

- Knowing, formulating, and accepting the rules and norms for being together helps reduce our conflicts.

Researchers have learned a lot about how to form groups and keep them together to make the world a better place. Our challenge is to continue learning more about community building and to help others by modeling the best of what we know.

How Does It All Fit Together?

In many parts of the country, rapidly increasing deer populations have surpassed the numbers present when Europeans began to migrate across North America. Large populations of deer can diminish forest and other vegetation to the point where they slowly starve. They can also create problems for people by eating crops and gardens and running into the paths of oncoming vehicles. Human attitudes toward deer quickly change from "love for Bambi's brothers and sisters" to "hate and fear of a four-legged menace" because of the damage and destruction they cause. How might a suburban community deal with this dilemma centered in a local forest preserve?

At a city council meeting, concerned citizens might express a variety of beliefs, attitudes, and values:

"There are too many deer. Let's get rid of them."

"I've hit two deer this year and the damage to my car amounts to more than $10,000. No deer is worth that much."

"I enjoy feeding and seeing deer. Let's not do anything."

"Let's live-trap them and move them out into the rural areas."

"Deer can be temporarily sterilized by feeding them a chemical. That would solve the population explosion problem."

"I'm a hunter and I could harvest some of the herd and donate the meat to the poor."

"If the people in town increase in number, would you shoot them, too? Let the deer be."

"Just let the deer alone. Population fluctuations are natural and their numbers will drop when the food supply is reduced."

"I raise vegetables for a living and the deer are ruining my business."

"Killing deer would be cruel because they feel pain like you and I do."

These types of responses and others could continue long into the night. The city council is asked to do its job and make the right decision in the matter. How can that be done when the worldviews expressed are so varied? What is the most ethical solution to the deer issue? How should the council decide?

This example of environmental ethics in action illustrates how input is needed from a variety of sources in a democratic society. Accurate information from ecologists, land managers, philosophers, and economists, to mention only a few, is necessary. Terminology must be clearly defined, including *overpopulation, natural, harvest,* and *cruel.* Various technologies for reducing the herd should be considered and evaluated for effectiveness, cost, and humane treatment of the animals.

The city council could limit public input and make the final decision based on the needs of the power structure and not the needs of all segments of the community. Even though the democratic process usually depends upon the power of the vote, is it possible that a minority group might have the most ethical solution? How could they convince the majority that they are right and their solution is the best? Does this deer issue demonstrate the complexity of making ethical choices after hearing from all interested parties and from those who have access to the best knowledge?

Another definition of ecology is the study of the structure and function of nature. Ecologists investigate communities in nature using established methods of science, and consider human as well as nonhuman nature.

As early as 1937, Aldo Leopold wrote about the importance of teaching ecological subject matter (along with taxonomy and natural history) in wildlife conservation courses. Harold Hungerford and Trudi L. Volk, both university researchers and science educators, identify ecological foundations as one of the recommended competency areas for environmental educators. This competency includes the ability to apply knowledge of key ecological principles and concepts in analyzing environmental issues. This ecology content includes understanding individuals, populations, communities, and ecosystems as well as the energy flows and cycles occurring in and among them.[57]

Some educators believe that ecological systems can serve as models for conducting human activities. Cheryl Charles points to characteristics of natural systems such as diversity of organisms and the roles they play (niches), self-regulation through systems of checks and balances, and the value of competing and cooperating organisms. She suggests such systems can serve as useful models for living in human communities.[58]

The use of technology impacts ecosystems as well as the long-term quality of life in human communities. The availability of nature's resources determines the technologies humans can invent. Although various technologies help humans meet their needs and wants, people need to become more aware of how their technologies affect the environment. For example, whenever humans convert nature into useful products, matter and energy is extracted from some ecosystem, sometimes never to return in a usable form. Knowing this allows us to better distinguish appropriate from inappropriate uses. Our technology choices directly affect both community life and enjoyment of nature.

Most people with biocentric worldviews believe people are distanced from the rest of nature by machines, reducing the quality of life. Yet, humans can also save endangered species with improved technology, reversing some of the negative impacts on habitats. Technologies can have negative impacts on local economies, such as when industrial technologies pollute a community, reducing property values. Transportation technology in the form of automobiles can improve people's access to natural areas while at the same time resulting in acid precipitation, which can affect the quality of lakes and forests used for outdoor education or recreation. Other technologies that help disseminate information and promote knowledge can affect how people live in human communities.

Ecology, nature, environment, technology, and community are all interconnected and affect one another and our lives. Barry Commoner's simplified Laws of Ecology can help us understand some of these relationships:

1. Everything is connected to everything else.

2. Everything must go somewhere.

3. Nature knows best.

4. There is no such thing as a free lunch.[59]

Does American society behave as though it believes in these laws? Do we act as though Earth matters? Does every person act on the basis of an environmental ethic of some kind, or do some people lack one?

Some would say everybody lives out a particular worldview reflecting some type of response toward nature and human nature. They would say everyone has an environmental ethic. However, philosopher Karen Warren disagrees. She makes it clear that a meaningful definition of environmental ethics does not include just any way of relating to the Earth. She believes "that ethical positions which are centered *only* on what is best for present and future generations of humans, or ones which explicitly deny that nonhumans are morally considerable, do not constitute an 'environmental ethic'."[60]

Notes

[1] Ernst Haeckel's book was titled *General Morphlogy of Organisms* (n.p., 1866). For more information about Haeckel, read Anna Bramwell, *Ecology in the 20th Century: A History* (New Haven, CT: Yale University Press, 1989).

[2] Edward O. Wilson, *Naturalist* (Washington, DC: Island Press/Shearwater Books, 1994), 363.

[3] Stephen R. Kellert, *Kinship to Mastery: Biophilia in Human Evolution and Development* (Washington, DC: Island Press, 1997), 175.

[4] Some dictionaries list up to 20 definitions for the adjective *natural* and up to 13 for the noun form.

[5] American Geological Institute, *Essence I*, rev. ed. (New York: Addison-Wesley, 1971).

[6] Bill McKibben, *The End of Nature* (New York: Random House, 1989), 65, 96.

[7] Neil Evernden, *The Social Creation of Nature* (Baltimore: Johns Hopkins University Press, 1992), xi.

[8] Ibid., 56, 84.

[9] Ibid., 21, 39; Rachel Kaplan and Stephen Kaplan, *The Experience of Nature: A Psychological Perspective* (New York: Cambridge University Press, 1989), 3.

[10] Evernden, *Social Creation of Nature*, 100.

[11] Holmes Rolston III, "Valuing Wildlands," *Environmental Ethics* 7 (spring 1985): 27-40.

[12] Clifford Knapp, "Images of Nature," *Nature Study* 45 (June 1992): 44-47.

[13] United Nations Environment Program, *World Charter for Nature* (Paris: United Nations Environment Program, 1982), 1.

[14] Nash, *The Rights of Nature*, 179.

[15] Details of their findings appear in Willett Kempton, James S. Boster, and Jennifer A. Hartley, *Environmental Values in American Culture* (Cambridge, MA: MIT Press, 1996), 39-62.

[16] Ibid., 40-43.

[17] Ibid., 49-53.

[18] Ibid., 54-55.

[19] Ibid., 55-56.

[20] Ibid., 57-60.

[21] Ibid., 62.

[22] Ibid., 202-205.

[23] *The Economist*, 17 January 1998, 26.

[24] Wendell Berry, *Home Economics: Fourteen Essays* (San Francisco: North Point Press, 1987), 146; David W. Orr, *Ecological Literacy: Education and the Transition to a Postmodern World* (Albany: State University Press of New York, 1992), 91.

[25] Neil Postman, *Technopoly: The Surrender of Culture to Technology* (New York: Knopf, 1992), 191.

[26] Baltic, "Technology and the Evolution of Land Ethics," 264-65.

[27] Clifford Stoll, *Silicon Snake Oil: Second Thoughts on the Information Highway* (New York: Doubleday, 1995), 11.

[28] Ibid., 3, 14, 26-27.

[29] Aldo Leopold, *A Sand County Almanac and Sketches Here and There* (New York: Oxford University Press, 1949), 158.

[30] Joseph Roggenbuck and B. L. Driver, "Public Land Management Agen-

cies, Environmental Education, and an Expanded Land Management Ethic," in *Nature and the Human Spirit,* ed. B. L. Driver, Daniel Dustin, Tony Baltic, Gary Elsner, and George Peterson (State College, Pa.: Venture Publishing, 1996), 383.

³¹ Richard J. Wilke, ed., *Environmental Education Teacher Resource Handbook: A Practical Guide for K-12 Environmental Education* (Millwood, NY: Kraus International Publications, 1993), 35.

³² *Clearing* is distributed by Creative Educational Networks, Oregon City, Oregon, telephone 503-657-6958, extension 2638. Read about other present-day educators who support developing an environmental ethic as part of the goal of environmental education (ethic as process) in David C. Engleson and Dennis H. Yockers, *Environmental Education: A Guide to Curriculum Planning,* 2d ed., Bulletin 94371 (Madison: Wisconsin State Department of Public Education, 1994), 34-40; Peter B. Corcoran and Eric Sievers, "Reconceptualizing Environmental Education: Five Possibilities," *Journal of Environmental Education* 25 (summer 1994): 8; and Mike Weilbacher, "The Single Most Important Thing to Know about the Earth (and It's Probably Not What You Think)," *Clearing* 85 (September/October 1994): 4.

³³ National Environmental Education Advisory Council, *Report Assessing Environmental Education in the United States and the Implementation of the National Environmental Education Act of 1990* (Washington, DC: U.S. Environmental Protection Agency, Environmental Education Division, 1996), 1.

³⁴ *Federal Register* 62 (22 August 1997).

³⁵ Edgar W. Jenkins, "Gender and Science & Technology Education," *Connect UNESCO International Science, Technology & Environmental Education Newsletter* 22 (1997): 1; *Rockford Register Star,* 20 April 1997, 3A.

³⁶ Al Gore, *Earth in the Balance: Ecology and the Human Spirit* (Boston: Houghton Mifflin, 1992; reprint, New York: Plume, 1993), 203; Richard Riley, "Closing the Distance," *Teaching pre-K-8* 28 (January 1998): 6.

³⁷ Works by these authors include Theodore Roszak, *The Voice of the Earth* (New York: Simon & Schuster, 1992); Jerry Mander, *In the Absence of Sacred: The Failure of Technology and the Survival of the Indian Nations* (San Francisco: Sierra Club Books, 1991); Postman, *Technopoly;* Postman, *The End of Education: Redefining the Value of School* (New York: Knopf, 1995); C. A. Bowers, *Educating for an Ecologically Sustainable Culture: Rethinking Moral Education, Creativity, Intelligence, and other Modern Orthodoxies* (Albany: State University of New York Press, 1995); Paul L. Wachtel, *The Poverty of Affluence: A Psychological Portrait of the American Way of Life* (New York: Free Press, 1983); David Strong, *Crazy Mountains: Learning from Wilderness to Weigh Technology* (Albany: State University of New York Press, 1995); and Gregory A. Smith, *Education and the Environment: Learning to Live with Limits* (Albany: State University of New York Press, 1992). For additional authors, see Orr, *Ecological Literacy,* reference and bibliography.

³⁸ *Rockford Register Star,* 25 February 1997; 7 December 1997; 17 December 1997; 12 March 1997; 14 September 1997; 22 July 1997; 10 September 1997; 1 June 1997.

[39] Robert Cwiklik, ed., "Class Wars: Are Computers the Saviors of Education? It Depends on Whom You Ask," *The Wall Street Journal*, 17 November 1997, R32.

[40] Ibid., R35.

[41] W. J. Rohwedder and Andy Alm, *Using Computers in Environmental Education: Interactive Multimedia and On-Line Learning* (Ann Arbor: Michigan University School of Natural Resources and Environmental, National Consortium for Environmental Education and Training, 1994), 1, 4-7.

[42] Susan Staniforth, *The Technology Trap, Module 1 Transportation: Who's in the Driver's Seat?* (Victoria, British Columbia: Sierra Club of British Columbia, Salvadoran Centre for Appropriate Technology, 1997), 1-2.

[43] Postman, *Technopoly*, 5.

[44] M. Scott Peck, *The Different Drum: Community-Making and Peace* (New York: Simon & Schuster, 1987), 62.

[45] Joel Westheimer and Joseph Kahne, "Building School Communities: An Experience-Based Model," *Phi Delta Kappan* 75 (December 1993): 325.

[46] John W. Gardner, *Building Community* (Washington, DC: Leadership Studies Program of Independent Sector, 1991), 14-29.

[47] Cheryl Charles, "Creating Community: What Is It and How Do We Do It? The Emerging Story of the Center for the Study of Community" (paper presented at the Eighth International Conference of the International Association for the Study of Cooperation in Education, Lewis and Clark College, Portland, OR, 10 July 1994), 7-9.

[48] Thomas J. Sergiovanni, *Building Community in Schools* (San Francisco: Jossey-Bass, 1994), 6. Ferdinand Tönnies's original work *Gemeinschaft and Gesellschaft* (Leipzig: Fues, 1887) was translated and edited by C. P. Loomis under the title *Community and Society* (East Lansing: Michigan State University, 1957; reprint, New Brunswick, NJ: Transaction Books, 1988).

[49] Sergiovanni, *Building Community in Schools*, 6, 8; Robert N. Bellah, Richard Madsen, William M. Sullivan, Ann Swidler, and Stephen M. Tipton, *Habits of the Heart: Individualism and Commitment in American Life* (Berkeley: University of California Press, 1985; updated with a new introduction, Berkeley: University of California Press, 1996).

[50] Sergiovanni, *Building Community in Schools*, 13.

[51] For examples, see Alan Thein Durning, *This Place on Earth: Home and the Practice of Permanence* (Seattle: Sasquatch Books, 1996); Tony Hiss, *The Experience of Place* (New York: Knopf, 1990; reprint, New York: Vintage Books, 1991); Gary Paul Nabhan and Stephen Trimble, *The Geography of Childhood: Why Children Need Wild Places* (Boston: Beacon Press, 1994); David Sobel, *Children's Special Places: Exploring the Role of Forts, Dens, and Bush Houses in Middle Childhood* (Tucson: Zephyr Press, 1993); and James A. Swan, *Nature as Teacher and Healer: How to Reawaken Your Connection with Nature* (New York: Villard Books, 1992).

[52] Roland L. Warren, "The Good Community—What Would It Be?" in *Perspectives on the American Community*, 2d ed., ed. Roland L. Warren (Chicago: Rand McNally, 1973), 467-77.

[53] Joseph Reimer, Diana Pritchard Paolitto, and Richard H. Hersh, *Promoting Moral Growth: From Piaget to Kohlberg*, 2d ed. (New York: Longman, 1983), 238. For a good overview of Kohlberg's philosophy, see Lawrence Kohlberg, "Stages of Moral Development as a Basis for Moral Education," in *Moral Education: Interdisciplinary Approaches*, ed. C. M. Beck, B. S. Critenden, and E. V. Sullivan (Toronto: University of Toronto Press, 1971); Kohlberg, "Continuities in Childhood and Adult Moral Development Revisited," in *Life-Span Developmental Psychology: Personality and Socialization*, ed. Paul B. Baltes and K. Warner Schaie (New York: Academic Press, 1973).

[54] Reimer, Paolitto, and Hersh, *Promoting Moral Growth*, 238-39.

[55] Ibid., 241.

[56] Ibid., 246.

[57] Leopold, "Teaching Wildlife Conservation in Public Schools," *Transactions of the Wisconsin Academy of Sciences, Arts, and Letters* 30 (1937): 77-78; Harold Hungerford and Trudi L. Volk, "The Challenges of K-12 Environmental Education," in *Monographs in Environmental Education and Environmental Studies, Volume I*, ed. Arthur B. Sacks (Columbus, OH: ERIC Clearinghouse for Science, Mathematics, and Environmental Education, 1984), 23-24.

[58] Charles, "Creating Community," 6.

[59] Barry Commoner, *The Closing Circle: Confronting the Environmental Crisis* (London: Cape, 1972), 33-46.

[60] Warren, "Warren's Proposed Model," 11.

CHAPTER 3

How Is an Environmental Ethic Achieved?

[An environmental ethic] guides human experience of and relations with the natural world in pursuit of sustenance and well-being.
—Tony Baltic, "Technology and
the Evolution of Land Ethics"

[An environmental ethic] presents and defends a systematic and comprehensive account of the moral relations between human beings and their natural environment.
—Joseph R. DesJardins, *Environmental Ethics*

Classifying Types of Environmental Ethics

According to Gary Varner, most environmental educators recognize that an essential part of their mission is to develop an environmental ethic in students. But what constitutes an environmental ethic is understood in different ways. There are various schemes for classifying types of environmental ethics.[1]

Varner names four ethic types, beginning with *anthropocentri-*

cism—the view that when it comes to deciding what to do and how it affects the environment, only the interests of human beings matter.[2] In other words, the primary reason to preserve the environment is to benefit humans, and the main purpose for stopping environmental degradation is to minimize the harm to humans. For example, anthropocentrists would want to save endangered wildlife because the animals are pleasurable to observe or because they are useful for other purposes such as hunting or to place in zoos. Some philosophers consider this position to be an ethic *about* the environment and not an environmental ethic.

A second type of ethic is *sentientism*. People who hold this view might be called animal liberation or animal rights advocates. They believe moral interests or rights should be accorded only to those nonhumans capable of experiencing pleasure or pain. Sentientists are not always sure which animals should be protected because some species with simple nervous systems may not be able to feel pleasure or pain. A sentientist might argue against whale hunting because it is wrong to kill or cause suffering to this mammal, which obviously feels pain when harpooned.

A third type of environmental ethic, *biocentric individualism,* is held by people who think all animals—even those with simple nervous systems like clams, spiders, and insects—have interests or rights and deserve moral consideration. These individuals might prefer to capture mice in live traps and release them outside the house instead of killing them. They might also allow biting mosquitoes to drink their blood rather than slap and kill them.

A fourth type of environmental ethic is *holism*. People with holistic ethics focus on the welfare of systems of living things rather than individual animals. Their viewpoint values the whole as more important than the sum of its parts. For example, a holist might favor caging the last free-flying California condors to breed them in captivity to save the species for possible reintroduction. Holists might also become active in restoring specific habitats such as prairies, savannas, or wetlands.[3]

These four ethic types described by Varner help distinguish a range along a human-centered vs. Earth-centered continuum. With this knowledge, educators can better evaluate current materials in their search for balance and fairness across a variety of ethic types and conduct activities representing a broader range of perspectives.

Bruce E. Matthews and Cheryl K. Riley add a fifth type, the *theocentrism* or God-centered view. Theocentrists believe they have a duty with respect to nature because it was created by God. They also believe that God requires humans to be Earth caretakers and consider abusing the Earth disrespectful. Matthews and Riley explain, "Environmental ethics asks the degree to which we value nature and why we do so, as we make choices about how we live within Earth's ecosystem." All five ethic types represent partial responses to the question: Why do we value nature?[4]

In a different classification scheme, William Frankena identifies eight types of environmental ethics. His classification system examines which facts are used to determine what is morally acceptable.

Ethical egoism considers facts related only to self-interest. Some philosophers would not regard this as an environmental ethic because it ranks humans first and gives nonhuman nature no moral priority.

Humanism or *personalism* considers facts related only to human beings. Most philosophers do not view animals, plants, air, and rocks as persons. These things have no moral status except as they relate to human needs or wants.

Sentientism considers facts related to beings that are aware of sensation and have the capacity to suffer or feel pleasure.

Reverence for life considers facts related to beings that are alive.

Planetary altruism considers facts related directly or indirectly to everything on the planet. There are two types of planetary altruists: individual beings are considered valuable in and of themselves, and the collection of individual beings that form systems is considered valuable as a whole.

The *theistic view* considers facts related to or about God.

Combination comprises any combination of two or more of the above pure types.

Cooperate with and follow nature considers facts related to and in agreement with nature and natural law.[5]

Educators in public schools and other secular organizations may find the theocentric or theistic view particularly challenging to discuss. Governmental guidelines for teaching *about* religion in public institutions are sometimes unclear, and public sentiment on this issue varies from community to community. A recent poll by The Pew Research Center revealed 71 percent of the respondents never doubt the existence of God (up from 60 percent in 1987). This may mean that the theocentric view will be challenged by students (and community members) less frequently than some others. The sentientist and the reverence-for-life views might be expected to provoke more community controversy than a God-centered view.[6]

David C. Engleson and Dennis H. Yockers recognize the importance of developing an environmental ethic in students. Using Bloom's Taxonomy of Educational Objectives for the Affective Domain, they identified examples of learner outcomes for the following categories: responding, valuing, organization, and characterization by value or value complex. For instance, they list two learner outcomes for the characterization category: "The student will develop a code of environmental behavior based on ethical principles consistent with maintaining the integrity of Earth" and "the student will develop a philosophy of life consistent with the role of humans as equal but not dominant members of the community composed of Earth and all its living things."[7]

By now you probably realize that the terms *Earth, nature, land,* and *ecosystems* are often used interchangeably with *environment.* Likewise, there are several synonyms in the *environmental ethics* literature: *land management ethic, ethic of ecosystem sustainability, conservation ethic, preservation ethic, wise use management ethic,* and *wilderness ethic.*[8] Several other related terms have appeared in print, such as *outdoor ethic, stewardship ethic, ethic of place, ecological consciousness,* and *Earth ethic.*

Gary Machlis thinks an *outdoor ethic* should grapple with three main issues:

1. It should be fully proposed, be carefully thought out and argued (reasonable men and women should be able to understand it), be attainable (earnest attempts to follow it should be successful), give specific direction to individual outdoor behaviors, contain a minimum of contradictions, and fit with generally accepted American values such as individualism and fairness.

2. It must deal directly with thorny issues such as defining who should have defendable moral interests—contemporary persons, future generations, corporations, Indian tribes, individual animals, species, habitats, ecosystems, or

other entities. It must consider responsibilities as well as rights. For example, do hunters have the right to a successful hunt, and if so, what are hunters' responsibilities to help perpetuate what they hunt?

3. It must address a broad scope and offer a wide vision, addressing topics such as how an American outdoor ethic will guide our behavior internationally.[9]

Stephen R. Kellert draws two conclusions about developing an environmental ethic. First, it requires "a fundamental sense of affection for and identification with nature, and a related capacity to perceive oneself as an integral and obligate member of the ecological community." Second, "unethical behavior is often associated with feelings of alienation and apartness from nature, allowing oneself to abuse and exploit the biota for various egoistic needs and immediate gratifications divorced from feelings of personal guilt or long-term responsibility."[10]

Kellert thinks nature must be meaningful on three levels. First, on the *affective (emotional) level*, people must have feelings of affection for and pleasure derived from direct contacts with nature. Second, on the *cognitive (intellectual) level*, individuals must have knowledge of the environment, including an enhanced appreciation of the biological and ecological characteristics of nature, as well as feelings of control and self-reliance when in natural settings. Third, on the *evaluative (beliefs and values) level*, people must have feelings of membership and identification with the ecological community.

Another way to understand how to help students develop an environmental ethic is to look for what is lacking when someone is judged not to have one. Kellert believes an individual lacking an environmental ethic would have diminished emotional identification with nature and would place short-term needs over long-term obligations to the ecological community. Nature would be viewed as separate, alien, and lacking in inherent value or integrity. It would be viewed as inanimate and something to be manipulated and exploited. Nature would be seen only as a means for displacing anger (e.g., by killing animals or destroying plants without cause) or achieving material gain (e.g., by selling a rare plant to decorate a bouquet, even though it was a threatened species) without regard for other humans or the biosphere.[11]

Living In Our Modern World

G. Tyler Miller, Jr. suggests most people use four excuses for not following an environmental ethic. First, there is gloom-and-doom pessimism. These people believe the world will come to an end anyway, so there is no point in making sacrifices for a healthier environment. A second excuse is blind technological optimism. This is the belief that human intelligence will always be able to develop new technologies to solve ecological problems. Fatalism, the third excuse, is the belief that we have no control over the direction of society and consequently can make little difference in society's use of resources. The last excuse is extrapolation to infinity. These people believe, "If I can't change the entire world quickly, I won't try to change any of it."[12]

Mohandas K. (Mahatma) Gandhi and Margaret Mead had responses to these excuses. Gandhi said, "Almost anything you do will seem insignificant, but it is very important that you do it." Mead's often-quoted affirmation complements Gandhi's: "Never doubt that a small group of committed citizens can change the world. Indeed, it is the only thing that has."

Milton McClaren, professor at Simon Fraser University, identified four flaws in the way humans think about the environment and themselves. His basic assumption is that environmental problems are the symptoms of faulty thinking. He contends that school curricula currently perpetuate these thinking flaws.

The first flaw equates economic growth with progress and goodness. People assume that everything done in the realm of commerce is sustainable and that a healthy economy requires a three to four percent annual increase in the gross economic product. McClaren suggests that to correct this flaw, our economic decisions must be based on principles derived from how natural systems operate.

The second flaw assumes technology and science will help humanity solve all environmental problems without requiring individuals to make personal sacrifices. He characterizes this way of thinking as belief in a "technological fix." An associated, erroneous belief is that information automatically compiles itself into an action plan. He points to critics who call for more research before acting on problems such as acid precipitation or global warming. He concludes that research information can only suggest possible human action. People must still decide among possible alternatives before choosing the most responsible action. A decision not to act on problems *is* a decision—and sometimes a risky one.

Another flaw in our thinking is caused by the confusing differences among number, quantity, quality, and value. McClaren points out that quality and value are related because they involve subjective judgments of attributes such as beauty, strength, and durability. The problem lies in believing that everything can be counted or that it should be. Intangibles such as clean air or scenic views are complex concepts that are difficult to quantify. In McClaren's opinion, schools have not done a very good job of clearing up the confusion. Some essential components of an environmental ethic, such as empathy for living things or respect for ecosystems, cannot be measured by using standardized tests or measurements.

Finally, McClaren looks at humanity's view of its place in nature and its current level of scientific understanding. The tendency for people to separate themselves from the laws that govern how ecosystems work is the result of flawed thinking, according to McClaren. Science arbitrarily creates boundaries and rules and then attempts to isolate the components of nature. This thinking flaw is based on the false idea that nature is simply the sum of its separate parts.[13]

As discussed earlier, there are many varieties of environmental ethics, ranging from very human-centered to very Earth-centered perspectives. Most of us hold ethics that are somewhere in the middle on this continuum. We also might find that we shift from place to place along this line depending upon the situation or conditions. People who are serious about developing an environmental ethic attempt to minimize the inconsistencies between what they say they value and how they live.

It is important to recognize that developing and living by an environmental ethic takes us on a lifelong path that is often uphill. Although living in modern society makes it difficult to minimize our negative impact on the Earth's systems, it is important not to get discouraged when we fall short of our ideals. We simply must use our environmental ethic as a guide and put one foot in front of the other.

Specific Environmental Ethics

The next few pages present more detailed summaries of some of the environmental ethics found in the literature. To understand more about each one, you may want to read the original sources. Each ethic represents a general orientation to nature. They are arranged here in an order that approximates a transition from a human-centered to an Earth-centered worldview.

Wise Use movement. The beliefs, attitudes, values, and principles associated with the Wise Use movement do not constitute an environmental ethic, according to many observers, because the guidance they provide for action is based exclusively on human considerations. This use of the term *wise use* is an interpretation of a philosophy promoted by Gifford Pinchot, the founder of professional forestry in the United States, who lived from 1865 to 1946.[14] Pinchot encouraged the wise use of natural resources for human benefit. Today's Wise Use movement constituency consists of a loosely knit organization of more than 250 groups dedicated to privatizing public lands. Their goals include opening access to minerals and oil on protected lands, logging old-growth forests, reducing protection of endangered species, and eliminating restrictions on wetlands development.

All the resources of the forest reserves are for use, and this use must be brought about in a thoroughly prompt and businesslike manner, under such restrictions only as will insure the permanence of these resources.

—Gifford Pinchot, *Dreamers and Defenders*

Some environmental advocates characterize the movement as an attempt by radical utilitarian members of society to maintain consumer-oriented lifestyles by prioritizing the needs of the extractive industries and expanding the national economy. People making decisions based on the Wise Use movement perspective restrict moral consideration to that which directly benefits humans exclusively. They advocate private-property stewardship and using the market to develop and conserve scarce resources.[15]

Social ecology. The social ecology ethic has been developed mainly by Murray Bookchin, who promotes the idea that most eco-logical problems arise from social problems such as economic, eth-nic, cultural, and gender con-flicts. Bookchin believes that the way humans deal with one another as social beings is the key to addressing these prob-lems. Social ecologists assert that human domination of na-ture is clearly linked to humanity's tendency to domi-nate other humans. They be-lieve our treatment of nature is linked to how political and economic systems work; therefore, we must closely examine society's hierarchal structures.[16]

Humans act upon their en-vironments with consider-able technical foresight, however lacking that fore-sight may be in ecological re-spects.

—Murray Bookchin, "What Is Social Ecology?"

They acknowledge an existing ecological crisis that threatens the survival of life on Earth. They believe close relationships between culture and nature should be evaluated in local communities. By critically examining and changing presently harmful social struc-tures, we can begin to address serious ecological problems. This approach to change through local community participation repre-sents a societal challenge. It draws upon a variety of disciplines such as science, feminism, anthropology, and philosophy to critique antiecological trends and create more sustainable communities. People holding this ethic usually believe we should redesign social systems to lessen human impact on the socially constructed idea of nature.[17]

Ecofeminism. Ecofeminism has evolved from the writings of Jim Cheney, Elizabeth Dodson Gray, Susan Griffin, Ynestra King, Carolyn Merchant, and others.[18] They believe that the oppression of both Earth and women are related historically and that all prejudice and discrimination (racism, sexism, and other "isms") must be elimi-nated to bring about the kind of ethical systems needed to achieve sustainability. Some consider ecofeminism a subset of social ecol-ogy, but others point to different historical sources and inspiration for the idea. Ecofeminism rejects hierarchal constructs, which often lead to domination, oppression, and abuse of human and nonhuman systems.

This ethic consists of three main philosophical ideas:

1. The Earth is sacred along with its inhabitants.

2. Humans and the Earth are intertwined, meaning that social justice is directly linked to caring for the Earth.

3. In using the Earth's resources, humans must also respect the Earth's natural cycles.

———————— ❧ ————————

Ecological feminism is the position that there are important connections—historical, experiential, symbolic, theoretical—between the domination of women and the domination of nature, an understanding of which is crucial to both feminism and environmental ethics.

—Karen Warren, "The Power and the Promise of Ecological Feminism"

———————— ❧ ————————

These three ideas reflect traditional wisdom—usually associated with tribal cultures all over the world—that ecofeminists want to reclaim.[19]

Ecofeminists, like other feminists, assign responsibility for our most pervasive ecological problems to patriarchal ways of thinking (manifested in modern technological development, industrialism, and militarism). Ecofeminists call for a new way of doing and being that eliminates dualisms, privilege, and dominance. They want women's relationships to the Earth acknowledged as sources of wisdom in decision making about land use and environmental quality planning. People holding this ethic usually believe we should make environmental policies by acknowledging the link between the domination of nature and the domination of women.

Stewardship/conservation/management. This land ethic is represented by people who believe humans should manage the land to benefit people *and* nonhuman nature. It is generally characterized by strong beliefs about taking care of the land and using it to satisfy human needs and wants. This view makes two key assumptions: the science of ecology can guide management decisions effectively, and humans have obligations to be caretakers (or stewards) and understand some of the laws governing how nature works. The needs of people take a high priority in making land management decisions as well as in preserving ecosystems. This is especially true when governmental agencies manage land for populations of game animals. Economics plays an important role in this world-view. Nature is seen primarily from the utilitarian standpoint of its use as a natural resource. The term *natural resource* implies nature is a commodity to preserve for use in various forms of recreation such

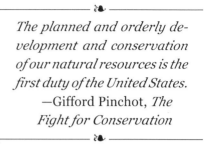

The planned and orderly development and conservation of our natural resources is the first duty of the United States.
—Gifford Pinchot, *The Fight for Conservation*

as hunting, fishing, trapping, hiking, and wildlife watching. Land also is cultivated to raise cattle or grow timber, grains, or other products for human consumption. Most of these human benefits can be represented in economic terms.

People holding this ethic usually believe we should use resources for the greatest good for the greatest number for the longest period of time. Some people who have adopted this view now work for state and federal agencies established primarily to manage natural resources for the public. By contacting the state departments of fish and game, conservation, or natural resources, you can request their written materials, which reflect this ethic.

Leopold's ecological conscience or land as community. Aldo Leopold thought humans should manage land while being members of the land community. According to his theory, preservation of the land's beauty and stability guides what is right and good to do. Leopold's idea of land includes more than the soil; it extends to plants, animals, water, air—what we now call the natural environment or ecosystem. He rejected the idea that the land should be viewed as property to be developed as expedient or necessary. He thought ethical land decisions should be based on perspectives broader than the economic.

Leopold defined an ethic in two ways: "An ethic, ecologically, is a limit on freedom of acting in the struggle for existence. An ethic, philosophically, is a differentiation of social from antisocial conduct." This means an ethic develops sequentially, originating in individuals working cooperatively rather than competing among themselves. As human populations and their use of more complex technologies increased, so did their cooperative behaviors.[20]

In his essay "The Land Ethic," published in *A Sand County Almanac*, Leopold suggested that modern humans lack a sense of moral obligation to preserve the land. He observed that humans view land mainly as they do other property—strictly from economic perspectives. Based on historical evidence, Leopold believed it was possible for societies to extend their ethics beyond human-to-human interactions to include respect for the land. He also thought this was an ecological necessity. Leopold wrote that "an ethic may be regarded as a mode of guidance for meeting ecological situations." Believing strongly that all people should have a land ethic, he criticized politicians and educators for not providing proper leadership. He was concerned that when humans assume the role of conqueror of land, they defeat themselves. He preferred that humans resume the role of plain citizen and take more responsibility for protecting the land.[21]

Ecology is the science of communities, and the ecological conscience is therefore the ethics of community life.

—Aldo Leopold, *The River of the Mother of God and other Essays by Aldo Leopold*

Leopold believed that an ethical relation to nature cannot "exist without love, respect, and admiration for land." He viewed the development of a land ethic as "an intellectual as well as emotional process." Leopold linked positive outdoor experiences with Earth-centered values: "No important change in ethics was ever accomplished without an internal change in our intellectual emphasis, loyalties, affections, and convictions."[22]

People holding this ethic usually adhere to the principle of preserving organisms by applying scientific knowledge and aesthetics to maintain the integrity of ecosystem functioning.[23]

Schweitzer's reverence for life. The ethic of reverence for life was developed mainly by Albert Schweitzer, who promoted the preservation of all life because of its inherent worth. He recognized how human existence conflicts with other lives on Earth and tried to resolve this tension. He valued all life including insects, amphibians, earthworms, and roadside flowers. Humans should cause pain or death in other beings, thought Schweitzer, only when faced with inescapable necessity. If people do take a life, they should try to compensate in some way for this loss.[24]

> *The time is coming, however, when people will be amazed that it took so long for mankind to recognize that thoughtless injury to life was incompatible with ethics.*
> —Albert Schweitzer,
> *Indian Thought and Its Development*

Schweitzer thought humans needed to develop their spiritual side and tell others about the need for protecting all life. He called his philosophy an ethic of love and respect. He equated being good with preserving and promoting life and being evil with destroying and mistreating life. He objected to using animals for sport or entertainment such as hunting, falconry, or bullfighting. Later in life, he stopped eating meat because of how the animals were raised.

He believed "everything that lives has value simply as a living thing" and defined ethics as "extended responsibility with regard to everything that has life." People holding this ethic usually believe all beings deserve life and our obligation is to preserve and treat it with respect.[25]

Deep ecology/bioregionalism. Deep ecology/bioregionalism was developed mainly by Arne Naess, a Norwegian philosopher, in the 1970s. It assigns independent value to all nonhuman life, suggesting humans should "live simply so that other life may simply live." The historical foundation for the movement is rooted in the writings of Henry David Thoreau, John Muir, Theodore Roszak, and Lewis Mumford, to mention only a few sources, as well as in many indigenous traditional beliefs. This ethic promotes societal changes by altering human perceptions, values, and behaviors. Deep ecologists and bioregionalists believe Western civilization is not dealing effectively with the increasing environmental degradation.

Naess distinguishes deep ecology from what he calls *shallow ecology*. Shallow ecology is largely human centered—concerned with pollution, resource depletion, and the effects of these on human health and affluence. Deep ecologists believe all human and nonhuman life has intrinsic value and that humans have no right to reduce this diversity, except to satisfy their vital needs.[26]

_____ ?⚘ _____

The well-being and flourishing of human and non-human life on Earth have value in themselves. . . . These values are independent of the usefulness of the non-human world for human purposes.
—Arne Naess, "The Deep Ecological Movement"

Bioregionalism upholds the hope of learning to live more lightly on the Earth, of developing communities integrated with their local ecosystems—creaturely associations that can carry the lifesome ethic forward through the generations.
—Stephanie Mills, *Home! A Bioregional Reader*

_____ ?⚘ _____

Deep ecologists think the Earth would benefit from fewer people and that Western society's predominant economic and technological policies should be changed through nonviolent global action. Deep ecologists believe they have an obligation to attempt to bring about these changes. Other terms that relate to this worldview are *bioregionalism, ecophilosophy, ecosophy, sustainable Earth ethics*, and *green philosophy and politics*. People holding this ethic usually believe that humans should question current political and economic policies, examine the underlying values of these policies, and learn as much as possible about their region in order to sustain themselves by consuming local products.[27]

Indigenous or traditional. This ethic has been developed by indigenous groups who have inhabited the Earth for thousands of years and continue to do so today. This view is represented in North America by writers such as Joseph Bruchac, Vine Deloria, Jr., Joy Harjo, N. Scott Momaday, Leslie M. Silko, and others. The ethic focuses on the interrelatedness of all Earth inhabitants—rocks, plants, water, and other entities—and the respect for their sacredness and power. In other words, moral objects should include nonhuman nature as well as humans. Despite the diversity among indigenous peoples around the world (in 1991 the United Nations estimated more than 300 million), many agree that certain themes run through most indigenous belief systems regarding nature.[28]

The Earth and its inhabitants are regarded as divine, and its people have a deep sense of reverence for nature. All Earth dwellers are believed to possess a spirit, and humans have a duty to protect them. This obligation to what they call the Mother Earth and the Creator involves expressing gratitude for the nurturing benefits humans receive. The land is considered a teacher, possessing wisdom about how to conduct the affairs of living in good ways. The natural world is viewed as alive, even the rocks, air, and streams; people should be involved in continuous dialogue with them. Human thoughts and feelings are closely intertwined with the processes of the universe, and the orderly and mysterious designs are celebrated through rituals and ceremonies. Elders are deeply respected for their wisdom, which is traditionally shared with others orally through meaningful stories.

Very old in the Native American worldview is the conviction that the Earth is vital, that there is a spiritual dimension to it, a dimension in which man rightly exists. It follows logically that there are ethical imperatives in this matter.

—N. Scott Momaday, "A First American Views His Land"

Indigenous people realize they need to kill plants and animals to live and offer sacred gifts such as corn, cedar, or tobacco in return. These people try to live their ethic of harmony with the rest of creation on a daily basis. People holding this ethic usually believe humans should treat all of nature as their kin—with respect and gratitude.[29]

Animal liberation and rights. Animal liberation has been developed primarily by Peter Singer, who advances the idea that because certain individual animals are capable of feeling pain, any act that causes their pain and suffering is wrong. Rights-based ethical views have been developed primarily by Tom Regan, who advocates assigning certain moral rights to individual animals and condemning any act that violates these rights. In other words, animals are considered moral objects.

The idea of liberating animals from mistreatment is a historical outgrowth of the liberation of slaves and women from oppression. The desire to extend moral rights to nonhumans is an extension of the idea of assigning rights to all people. The ethics of liberation and rights are related, but there are some differences in the underlying beliefs and values.

Singer outlined his thoughts on liberation in his book *Animal Liberation*. He believes in minimizing pain and discomfort for certain animals. If an animal is considered to feel pain (sentience), it should be given moral consideration. Determining which animals feel the most pain is critical to this decision. When conflicts arise in deciding which animals to protect, the right and good decision is based on the action that creates the most happiness for all concerned. Even though he does not think animals possess moral rights, he believes humans have moral duties to sentient animals. He believes it is wrong to discriminate against animals because of their particular species. In other words, the human animal should not claim any privilege not granted also to a nonhuman animal. Unequal treatment based on species is called *speciesism*, a concept used similarly to the ideas of racism and sexism.

Regan thinks animal rights should be protected through political processes, education, and the public media. His book *The Case for Animal Rights* calls for asking deep and probing questions about morality. He believes nonhuman animals and humans have

> *Animal liberation will require greater altruism on the part of mankind than any other liberation movement, since animals are incapable of demanding it for themselves, or of protesting against their exploitation by votes, demonstrations, or bombs.*
>
> —Peter Singer, *Animal Liberation*

> *I have argued that if humans have rights, so do many animals. . . . I have argued for what appears to be the most promising line of argument for explaining human rights, the view that we have inherent value and that this can rationally be extended to animals of some kinds.*
>
> —Tom Regan, "Animal Rights, Human Wrongs"

equal inherent value, but he isn't sure about the status of rocks, rivers, or trees. If society would fully adopt animal liberation or rights values, our lifestyles would have to change significantly. People holding this ethic usually believe that nonhuman animals should be protected from the abuses many societies accept as ethical practices, such as hunting, fishing, trapping, and raising most animals for food on mass scales.[30]

Radical ecoactivism. The term *radical* is derived from a Latin word meaning root. Any actions that get at the root of an ecological problem could be described as radical. Because some actions are more violent than others, this ethic is characterized by more extreme measures designed to promote change. Peter C. List categorizes ecological movements such as Greenpeace, The Sea Shepherd Society, Earth First!, The Earth Liberation Front, and the actions of the late Edward Abbey among others as radical. Although other ethics promote social change, the actions of these groups are often more direct and aggressive. People such as Abbey, Peter Berg, David Foreman, and Paul Watson come closest to holding and advocating this view.[31]

Perhaps all of them would agree with Thoreau, who wrote, "If . . . the machine of government is of such a nature that it requires you to be the agent of injustice to another, then, I say, break the law."[32] In this case, the "other" includes animals, plants, and whole ecosystems. Tactics used by radical ecoactivists range from disruptive, nonviolent civil disobedience (e.g., demonstrating or boycotting offensive products) to more aggressive methods (e.g., destroying road equipment, pulling out land survey stakes, spiking trees scheduled to be

> *Sentiment without action is the ruin of the soul. One brave deed is worth a thousand books.*
> —Edward Abbey, *A Voice Crying in the Wilderness*

> *We do not engage in radical action because we are primarily motivated by opposition to authority, . . . but because we are for something—the beauty, wisdom, and abundance of this living planet.*
> —David Foreman, *Confessions of an Eco-Warrior*

Perspectives on Human and Nonhuman Nature: A Continuum of Environmental Ethic Types

Human-Centered Worldview
As a person who is superior to nature, what can it do for me and how can I best control it?

▼

Wise Use Movement—Humans should have access to all natural areas because private property rights should ,take priority over public property rights. (Some philosophers do not consider this to be an environmental ethic.)

▼

Social Ecology and Justice—Humans should redesign social and political systems to help understand and address serious ecological problems.

▼

Ecofeminism—Humans should address the unequal status and oppression of women to understand better how patriarchal societies have treated nature in similar ways.

▼

Stewardship/Conservation/Ecomanagement—Humans should take responsibility for protecting ecosystems and their inhabitants so they can continue to be managed for society's benefit.

▼

Leopold's Ecological Conscience or Land As Community—Humans should use ecological knowledge to develop an ethic of respect and love in caring for natural communities.

timbered). The more violent tactics are known as *monkey-wrenching*, *ecoanarchy*, or *ecotage*. It is true that U.S. history records many instances of acting on ethical principles to bring about social and political reform. The Boston Tea Party is just one example.[33] When teaching about ecoactivism, however, educators should point out that many of these acts are unlawful and can end in violence.

Schweitzer's Reverence for Life—Humans should treat all organisms with deep respect, and if they must take a life, they should compensate for this loss in some way.

Deep Ecology/Bioregionalism—Humans should live simply to have a minimal impact on other Earth dwellers (which have value apart from their use by people) because all the planet's inhabitants deserve to reach self-realization.

Traditional or Indigenous—Humans should take daily responsibility for living in harmony and reciprocity with other sacred inhabitants of a nurturing and life-giving Mother Earth.

Animal Welfare/Rights—Humans should not harm other animals capable of feeling pain by performing experiments, killing them for sport, or raising them for food. Also, they should treat other animals as though they have the same rights as humans.

Radical Ecoactivism—If necessary, humans may use extreme measures, which do not injure other humans, to prevent individuals from harming nature, even if the tactics are illegal.

▼

Earth-Centered Worldview

As a person sharing equal status with the rest of nature,
how can I respect it?

What It Means

These environmental ethics, although appearing in different categories, share some overlapping beliefs, attitudes, values, and principles. They are based primarily on the writings and activities of individuals or groups of people who have promoted them. They span the human-centered/Earth-centered continuum. They are presented here to give the reader an overview of some of the basic ethics held by people identifying with each.

Because of this wide range of environmental ethics, it is not always an easy process simply to define one's single position. People can be eclectic and choose beliefs, attitudes, values, and principles from several. If educators truly believe in exposing students to a range of ethic alternatives, these descriptions provide a starting place.

Notes

[1] Gary Varner, "The Role of Environmental Ethics in Environmental Education," in *Environmental Ethics: Strategies for Implementation—Nonformal Workshop*, ed. C. H. Yaple (Orlando, FL: National Association for Environmental Education, 1988), 1.

[2] Ibid.

[3] Ibid., 2.

[4] Bruce E. Matthews and Cheryl K. Riley, *Teaching and Evaluating Outdoor Ethics Education Programs* (Vienna, VA: National Wildlife Federation, 1995), 105, 125.

[5] William K. Frankena, "Ethics and the Environment," in *Ethics and Problems of the 21st Century*, ed. K. E. Goodpaster and K. M. Sayre (Notre Dame, IN: University of Notre Dame Press, 1979), 3-20.

[6] *Rockford Register Star*, "Belief in God on Upswing," 22 December 1997, 6A.

[7] Engleson and Yockers, *Guide to Curriculum Planning*, 39-40.

[8] Roggenbuck and Driver, in *Nature and the Human Spirit*, 383-402.

[9] Gary Machlis, "Outdoor Ethics in America," in *Proceedings of the International Conference on Outdoor Ethics* (Arlington, VA: Izaak Walton League of America, 1987), 13-14.

[10] Stephen R. Kellert, "Social and Psychological Dimensions of an Environmental Ethic," in *International Conference on Outdoor Ethics*, 19.

[11] Ibid., 18.

[12] Miller, *Living in the Environment*, 592.

[13] Milton McClaren, "After Earth Day 1990 . . . What?" in *The Best of Clearing: Environmental Education in the Pacific Northwest, Vol. IV*, ed. Larry Beutler (Oregon City, OR: The Environmental Project, 1993), 31-32.

[14] To read more about Pinchot, see Gifford Pinchot, *Breaking New Ground* (1947; reprint, Washington, DC: Island Press, 1998); Douglas H. Strong, *Dream-*

ers and Defenders: American Conservationists (Lincoln: University of Nebraska Press, 1988).

[15] Driver et al., *Nature and the Human Spirit*, 241. To learn more about the Wise Use movement perspective, contact Foundation for Research on Economics and the Environment, 502 South 19th Avenue, Suite 5, Bozeman, MT 59715 and Committee for a Constructive Tomorrow, P.O. Box 65722, Washington, DC 20035.

[16] Michael Zimmerman, ed., *Environmental Philosophy: From Animal Rights to Radical Ecology* (Englewood Cliffs, NJ: Prentice Hall, 1993), 25. Zimmerman's excellent book provides overviews of many of the environmental ethic types (e.g., animal rights and welfare, land ethic, deep ecology, ecofeminism, and social ecology).

[17] For more information, write the Institute for Social Ecology, P.O. Box 89, Plainfield, VT 05667.

[18] Works by these authors include Jim Cheney, "Eco-Feminism and Deep Ecology," *Environmental Ethics* 9 (summer 1987): 115-45; Gray, "Come Inside the Circle of Creation"; Ynestra King, "Healing the Wounds: Feminism, Ecology, and the Nature/Culture Dualism," in *Reweaving the World: The Emergence of Ecofeminism*, ed. Irene Diamond and Gloria Feman Orenstein (San Francisco: Sierra Club Books, 1990); and Carolyn Merchant, "Ecofeminism and Feminist Theory," in *Reweaving the World*.

[19] Diamond and Orenstein, *Reweaving the World*, xi-xii.

[20] Leopold, *Sand County Almanac*, 202.

[21] Ibid., 203.

[22] Ibid., 223, 225, 209-10.

[23] For further information, contact the Aldo Leopold Foundation, Inc., E-12919 Levee Road, Baraboo, WI 53913.

[24] Ann Cottrell Free, ed., *Animals, Nature, and Albert Schweitzer* (New York: A. Schweitzer Fellowship, 1982), 6.

[25] Nash, "Aldo Leopold's Intellectual Heritage," in *Companion to A Sand County Almanac: Interpretive & Critical Essays*, ed. J. Baird Callicott (Madison: University of Wisconsin Press, 1987), 50, 64. For further information about Schweitzer and his philosophy, write the Albert Schweitzer Center, Hurlburt Road, RD 1 Box 7, Great Barrington, MA 01230.

[26] George Sessions, ed., *Deep Ecology for the Twenty-First Century* (Boston: Shambhala, 1995), xii.

[27] For further information, write the Institute for Deep Ecology, P.O. Box 1050, Occidental, CA 95465 and the Planet Drum Foundation, P.O. Box 31251, San Francisco, CA 94131 (Shasta Bioregion, U.S.A.).

[28] Good resources for indigenous or traditional ethics include Joseph Bruchac, *Between Earth & Sky: Legends of Native American Sacred Places* (San Diego: Harcourt Brace & Co., 1996); Vine Deloria, Jr., *God Is Red: A Native View of Religion*, 2d ed. (Golden, CO: North American Press, 1992); Joy Harjo, *Secrets from the Center of the World* (Tucson: University of Arizona Press, 1992);

Leslie M. Silko, *Ceremony* (New York: Viking Press, 1977; reprint, New York: Penguin Books, 1986); Silko, *Storyteller* (New York: Seaver Books, 1981); Silko, *Almanac of the Dead: A Novel* (New York: Simon & Schuster, 1991); and David Suzuki and Peter Knudtson, *Wisdom of the Elders: Honoring Sacred Native Visions of Nature* (New York: Bantam Books, 1992).

[29] A good source for Native Americans who express this ethic is Karen D. Harvey, Lisa D. Harjo, and Lynda Welborn, *How to Teach about American Indians* (Westport, CT: Greenwood Press, 1995). It includes extensive bibliographic information.

[30] For further information, write the Animal Protection Institute, P.O. Box 22505, Sacramento, CA 95822 and the Animal Welfare Institute, P.O. Box 3650, Washington, DC 20007.

[31] Works by these authors include Peter C. List, ed., *Radical Environmentalism: Philosophy and Tactics* (Belmont, CA: Wadsworth, 1993); Edward Abbey, *Desert Solitaire: A Season in the Wilderness* (New York: McGraw Hill, 1968; reprint, New York: Simon & Schuster, 1990); Peter Berg, "More Than Just Saving What's Left," in *Home! A Bioregional Reader*, ed. Van Andruss, Christopher Plant, Judith Plant, and Eleanor Wright (Philadelphia: New Society Publishers, 1990); David Foreman, *Confessions of an Eco-Warrior* (New York: Harmony Books, 1991); Foreman, "The New Conservation Movement," in *Deep Ecology for the Twenty-First Century*; Paul Watson and Warren Rogers, *Sea Shepherd: My Fight for Whales and Seals*, ed. Joseph Newman (New York: Norton, 1982); and Paul Watson and Peter Dykstra, "Greenpeace," *Environment* 28 (July- August 1986): 45.

[32] Nash, *Rights of Nature*, 161.

[33] For further information, read *Earth First! The Radical Environmental Journal*, P.O. Box 1415, Eugene, OR 97440.

What Is Environmental Values and Ethics Education?

*Only the choices and tastes and judgments of healthy human
beings will tell us much about what is good for the human
species in the long run.*

—Abraham H. Maslow,
Toward a Psychology of Being

The field of values and moral education has been established in
the literature and in some schools since before the turn of the century. It has always been controversial but considered essential to the
development of youth. Within the broad field of values and moral
education lies Earth-centered values education. This chapter examines the historical context for values education, explores useful teaching strategies for developing an environmental ethic, and discusses
problems and promises in implementing these strategies.

Values and Ethics Education

Terminology can be confusing because different people assign
different meanings to many words. For purposes of this book, five
key terms must be defined: facts, beliefs, attitudes, values, and principles.

Facts are pieces of information that have objective reality; for example, it is fact that some apples are red. A person may claim something is factual, but the truth of the statement must be tested to determine its accuracy. Information is a collection of facts.

A *belief* is the conviction of the reality of some phenomenon, usually based on an examination of facts. For example, I believe water is made up of hydrogen and oxygen. Beliefs can be challenged, depending on the accuracy or comprehensiveness of the facts considered. A collection of related beliefs about a topic make up a belief system.

Attitudes are ideas used to evaluate something, either positively (for example, recycling glass and aluminum is good for the environment) or negatively (for example, litter along the roadside is ugly). Attitudes may or may not be reflected in a person's behavior. A collection of related attitudes about a topic makes up an attitudinal system.

Values are ideas about the worthiness of objects or activities. Values usually develop over a relatively long period of time. They tend to guide behavior and serve either as a means of reaching an end (instrumental value) or as an end in themselves (terminal value). For example, an instrumental value, driving a high gas mileage car, is a way to achieve a terminal value—saving money or fuel. Values can be arrived at after critically thinking about alternative responses and their consequences if acted upon. Some values are handed down from one generation to the next and are simply accepted. A value is reflected in a consistent behavioral pattern over time. A collection of related values makes up a value system. Values can also describe certain character traits that have long been considered worthwhile (virtues). Values such as respect, responsibility, compassion, loyalty, tolerance, open-mindedness, and others form the basis of a movement called *character education.* Difficulties arise when there is disagreement about the specific behaviors that constitute each trait. Problems also arise when two or more values conflict with one another, making it difficult to decide which to act on. According to Thomas Lickona, values are of two kinds. Nonmoral values express what we want or like to do (preferences), such as listening to classical music or reading a novel. Moral values tell us what we ought to do, such as acting honestly, responsibly, or fairly toward others.[1]

Principles are rules or standards for deciding how to order conflicting values (e.g., if a person values all living things and a sanitary kitchen, and a cockroach is discovered there, what rules or standards should apply in deciding what to do with the cockroach?). Principles that sort out how to act when values conflict can be called prioritizing principles.

How do these elements—facts, beliefs, attitudes, values, and prioritizing principles—relate to an environmental ethic? When all five elements are considered in personal lifestyle or community choices, opportunities for reaching ethical decisions increase. According to Timothy Beatley,

> Ethical land use takes existing personal values as an input to making ethical judgments; land-use ethics is the broader concern of making moral choices, applying ethical standards and principles to specific land-use dilemmas, and defending these moral judgments.[2]

The following diagram summarizes the relationships among these key terms.

Many Facts (Information)
form
▼
Fewer Beliefs,
which form
▼
Even Fewer Attitudes,
which form either
▼
Nonmoral Values (Preferences)
OR
Moral Values (Obligations),
which, when combined with
Prioritizing Principles,
▼
and Processed by Critical Thinking,
▼
Result in a Greater Probability of Making Ethical Choices

Throughout history, societies have been concerned about the values and morals of their people. Before formal institutions such as schools and churches were established, most youth learned the necessary values and morals from their families and communities. As societies became more structured, this role was shared by teachers and clergy. This has always been considered a responsibility of the school because values and morals are so important in allowing people to live together compatibly. Because of the importance placed on cultural, societal, and personal values, controversy frequently arises around what roles schools (especially public schools) should play in addressing values questions.

Values are human tendencies to act preferentially for one kind of object or objective over another.[3] Acting on values can involve various levels of conceptual thinking—from almost none to a great deal. Action can also involve feelings of different intensities. In other words, people can be very conscious of the rational bases on which they behave or barely conscious of the underlying reasons for their actions.

Moral values relate to principles of right and wrong behavior or good and bad character. A moral choice usually considers the impact of an action on self or others and judges the action according to a standard or set of standards.[4]

A belief refers to what people think the world is like, and a value refers to the guiding principles behind what is moral, desirable, or just. Michael J. Caduto defines an attitude as "a relatively enduring organization of beliefs around an object or situation predisposing one to respond in some manner." Caduto believes an adult has thousands of beliefs, fewer attitudes, and only dozens of values. Beliefs, attitudes, and values are organized by the brain within conceptual categories that reduce their complexity, which means this is all much simpler than it seems.[5]

Hunter Lewis developed a framework for describing how we choose and develop our values. He proposed that six different styles of thinking influence our ethical decisions: authority, logic, sense experience, emotion, intuition, and science. It helps to know the sources of our values if we want to modify or replace them with different ones.[6]

Howard Kirschenbaum combines the terms *values education* and *moral education* and defines it as "the conscious attempt to help others acquire the knowledge, skills, attitudes and values that contribute to more personally satisfying and socially constructive lives."[7]

He describes four major movements in the overall field of values education. The first, *values realization*, consists of a variety of approaches designed to help individuals determine, recognize, implement, and act upon their life values. *Values realization*, a term Sidney B. Simon coined in 1980, grew out of an earlier movement— *values clarification.* In this approach, the teacher facilitates the process of value formation instead of imposing specific values on students. This method is especially appropriate when discussing values dealing with personal preferences within the context of a diverse set of socially acceptable values.

The second movement is *character education.* Its major goal is to instill traditional values that promote virtuous and responsible conduct. Respect, reverence, compassion, self-discipline, and loyalty are examples of values to be nurtured in students.

Another category is *citizenship education*, which focuses on teaching civic values—those values necessary to support the maintenance of a participatory or representative democracy. Promoting the public good, individual rights, and justice are examples of basic values operating within a country's political and legal systems.

Moral education is the fourth category described by Kirschenbaum. It is designed to teach the necessary beliefs, attitudes, and values to become a good, fair, or kind person. Proponents of this movement teach students about the moral traditions, processes of moral reasoning, and values such as compassion and altruism in society.

From these brief descriptions, it is difficult to draw sharp distinctions among all the approaches, but they do vary in several important philosophical beliefs and practices. These movements are affected by the sociological, philosophical, and historical forces that shaped them. There are two important points to remember: historically, the teaching of values and morality was a significant reason for establishing educational institutions in the first place, and there is and always has been a broad range of opinion about how the process should be carried out.

Kirschenbaum favors the integration of several approaches. He advocates a comprehensive approach to values and moral education and suggests methods, strategies, techniques, and activities in his book *100 Ways to Enhance Values and Morality in Schools and Youth Settings*. This book takes the same selective approach, but the focus has been narrowed to environmental ethics (there is more to come on this topic later in the chapter).[8]

Kevin Ryan, in an article in the *Phi Delta Kappan*, outlined five approaches to teaching about values. He labeled them "the Five E's":

1. Teaching by *example* is modeling good behavior. If teachers think recycling glass and aluminum will save energy and subsequently protect the environment, they should set the example by doing this themselves at home and in school.

2. Teaching by *explanation* involves conveying important information about value formation and encouraging discussions about issues, rules, rights, and responsibilities. Explaining how industrial and automotive emissions can result in acid precipitation in distant places illustrates this approach.

3. Teaching by *exhortation* is the urging of certain moral directions. Ryan cautions that educators should use this approach sparingly and never stray far from explanation. Exhortation is controversial because if a teacher tries to promote a value that is not agreed upon by the majority of the community, people may become upset and label exhortation as indoctrination or brainwashing.

4. Creating an *environment* means encouraging respectful behavior and striving for high standards of human communication. Educators recognize that free expression and rational decisions are more likely to occur in communities of caring, civil individuals. This approach advocates creating a moral climate in which fairness and open discussion of ethical questions are the norms. When safe learning communities are established, values may be freely discussed and sometimes acted upon, while still respecting individual minority values.

5. Providing *experience* involves participating in meaningful activities that encourage feelings of competence and self-

esteem. People who perform meaningful services to the community such as planting trees or feeding birds often feel connected to something larger than themselves. They also see more clearly the links between their expressed values and their actions, especially if these actions are freely chosen because they are prized.[9]

Caduto outlined several valuing strategies that have been used in environmental values education. Selected for discussion in this book are inculcation, values clarification, values analysis, moral development, action (service) learning, and confluent education. Caduto also lists laissez-faire and behavior modification as separate strategies, but these will not be discussed here. Caduto admits that since laissez-faire is strictly a "hands off" policy, it is not considered a moral education strategy. Behavior modification techniques could be a contributing aspect of the inculcation approach and will not be treated separately here.[10]

Values Education Strategies

Inculcation. This strategy, equivalent to exhortation as used by Ryan, involves attempts to change the values of others in chosen directions. Methods include "moralizing" lectures, selected modeling, positive and negative reinforcement (behavior modification), and other techniques that describe or structure right and wrong behavior as prescribed by the individual teacher, program, or curriculum. Inculcation can safely take place in situations where the school and community have agreed upon a set of values they want students to hold and practice. This approach stops short of methods called brainwashing or indoctrinating, which occur under more authoritarian conditions. Students who are brainwashed or indoctrinated have no freedom to consider alternatives to what has been mandated as right or wrong.[11]

Values clarification. This strategy involves a variety of structured activities that allow the learner to consider three aspects of the valuing process: (1) choosing freely from alternatives after thoughtful consideration of the consequences, (2) prizing and cherishing the choice and publicly affirming it, and (3) acting in a repeated pattern in life situations. This strategy has now evolved into a broader approach known as *values realization*. Clarification of values can occur along with inculcation when educators are clear about which values the students are free to choose and which they must conform to because of community norms.[12]

Values analysis. This strategy involves the application of a rational, logical, problem-solving method to analyze social issues. Relevant facts are gathered, their truth is assessed, and a tentative value decision is reached and tested before a final position is taken. In some instances, the value decision is acted upon in the community. This strategy was originally developed by social studies educators, but other educators have now adopted these analytical and sequential methods.[13]

Moral development. This strategy primarily involves the use of moral dilemma or values-problem discussions based on contrived or real incidents. The strategy incorporates the developmental theories of Jean Piaget and Lawrence Kohlberg and considers how humans evolve in their abilities to make more complex moral judgments over time.[14]

Action learning. This strategy involves participating in direct, experiential learning through various "hands-on" projects. Sometimes called *service learning*, this strategy often provides a service to the community while students learn required academic knowledge. If these projects are not freely chosen and implemented by students, they might be considered a form of inculcation imposed by the teacher.[15]

Confluent learning. This strategy involves the integration of cognitive and affective awareness techniques using the senses. It is often presented in a democratic, student-directed teaching style. Examples of outdoor confluent activities include touching a tree while blindfolded, walking in a swamp, or empathizing with animals through role playing.[16]

Each of these six values strategies has strengths and weaknesses; *all* should be used in a comprehensive values education program. In many cases, they require different teaching styles, which in turn correspond to different learning styles of the students.

Bruce E. Matthews and Cheryl K. Riley completed an extensive study to identify effective outdoor ethics education. Although outdoor ethics is concerned, in part, with the well-being of nature, it is also obligated to consider people and their outdoor activities. Matthews and Riley examine the research in the broad area of values education and conclude that behavioral change resulting from values education can be attributed to

- the nurturing of certain behaviors in families, neighborhoods, and communities;
- teachers who serve as helpful guides rather than as authoritarians;
- groups that make decisions through consensus and help develop their own norms and codes of moral behavior;
- peer teaching, counseling, and support;
- responsible service and action strategies in the community.[17]

These findings encourage teachers to pursue ongoing comprehensive values education programs after building supportive learning communities and communicating their plans to the larger community.

Lickona also examined the formal research in values education. He criticized the validity of most current research but noted a few promising empirical studies. He cited one five-year study carried out in six elementary schools (grades K-4) by California's Child Development Project. Research designers posed the question: "Does a multi-faceted values program, begun in Kindergarten and sustained through a child's elementary school years, make a measurable and lasting difference in a child's moral thinking, attitudes, and behavior?"[18]

Significant differences between the control and experimental groups emerged in four areas. Children in the values education program

1. showed more spontaneous acts of helping, cooperating, caring, and encouraging others in the classroom;

2. showed more concern toward others on the playground, but were not less assertive than the control group;

3. paid more attention to the needs of all parties, were less likely to propose aggressive solutions, and came up with more alternative plans in resolving hypothetical conflicts;

4. were more committed to democratic values such as the belief that all group members have a right to participate in decision-making activities.[19]

All of these gains were achieved without sacrificing other more traditional academic goals.

Lickona's findings agree with the conclusions of Matthews and Riley in supporting comprehensive or multifaceted values education programs in supportive and caring communities over time.

Harold R. Hungerford, Trudi L. Volk, and their graduate students at Southern Illinois University have conducted one of the most significant, longitudinal, and empirical lines of research related to positive and responsible environmental action. Over a period of years, they have investigated the goals, guidelines, and critical components for developing effective environmental education curricula leading to responsible citizenship behavior in students. Their most valuable contribution for helping students form environmental values and ethics is a skills-development curriculum model for investigating and evaluating environmental issues. Further reference to Hungerford's model can be found later in this chapter.[20]

Teaching Environmental Values

An important question currently being debated among outdoor and environmental educators is whether teachers should advocate specific values promoting ecosystem sustainability and responsible behaviors in their students or simply present valid and accurate information so students can form their own conclusions. The answer relates closely to the role of action learning projects in the program. Some critics believe values should not be acted upon under the auspices of the school, while others think they should be. According to this book's definition of a value, action must be an integral part of values education.

Action projects should always be guided by a set of underlying beliefs, attitudes, and values. Environmental advocacy involves supporting projects that give wild nature high priority. Teachers who value healthy streams and forests should express this and explain how they reached their belief. This behavior provides a positive role model to students. If students then want to protect a stream's aquatic life from gasoline and oil runoff from a service station, they may choose to take corrective action. If they value wildlife, they may choose to plant trees in a park to attract animals. At the same time, teachers should also encourage and support the expression of alternative value perspectives. Teachers can be strong advocates for nature and still provide a safe community climate for discussing and acting upon different views. The precedent has already been set by values programs that inculcate communities' positions on AIDS awareness, antismoking and substance abuse campaigns, nonviolent conflict resolution, healthy eating habits, physical fitness, and racial equality.

Having community support for introducing controversial topics into school programs is essential. When board policies encourage discussion, debate, and action based on agreed-upon values, teachers can help students develop environmental ethics with less difficulty. This kind of support can also clarify the appropriate issues to introduce at various grade levels. Few people, for example, would support the study of the emotional and complex issue of sport hunting at the first-grade level.

According to Erich Loewy, a professor of bioethics at the University of California at Davis, people must be empowered to think through questions of right and wrong so they can arrive at their own answers. Educational problems arise in democratic societies when people have different views on what questions to ask and what answers to accept. Controversy in public education results when people cannot agree on the meaning of knowledge. Some view knowledge as value free and important only when used to answer a specific question. Others view knowledge as value laden and only significant when good knowledge is used to answer a question.

Loewy thinks the only way to deal effectively with ethical questions is to create a mature society capable of deliberating answers and making decisions democratically. He believes three conditions are necessary for democratic decision making: (1) a willingness to listen and debate while respecting different opinions, (2) an economic democracy in which hungry and homeless people do not constitute an underclass, and (3) an educational democracy in which everyone has the ability to pursue certain ideas. By Loewy's reckoning, people cannot make ethical choices without all three elements.[21]

Controversies can arise when communities disagree about what is factual, what methodologies are best for student learning, or what beliefs, attitudes, and values should be reflected in the curriculum. For example:

- When a community cannot decide on answers to questions related to global climate change such as, Does it exist and if so how is it caused? or What should be done about it? the public school curriculum can become controversial.

- When a community cannot decide whether or not students should become involved in citizen-action projects to protect or improve the environment, this method of instruction can become controversial.

- When a community cannot agree on key beliefs, attitudes, and values, schools tend to avoid dealing with important environmental issues.

- When a community cannot decide on values regarding natural environments that are contested by the power structure in the community, teachers are often accused of indoctrinating or brainwashing students (on the other hand, when public school educators attempt to inculcate environmental values that are accepted by the power structure in the community, they may be evaluated as good teachers and encouraged).

Good teachers are usually able to distinguish the accepted values from the contested values and challenge students of appropriate ages and developmental levels to examine critically the values at the intersection of these two opposing poles. One test for indoctrination is to ask the question: "Is it possible for a student to freely express a value different from one held by the teacher?" If the answer is yes, indoctrination has not occurred.

Milton McClaren suggests inventing a new word, *ethicating*, to describe the interplay of factors in choosing what is right, good, valuable, worthy of obligation or duty, or deserving of rights. The process of valuing (deciding what has worth) differs from the more complex process of ethicating (combining feelings, beliefs, attitudes, and values and prioritizing them according to certain principles before making choices). When students begin with a problem or issue involving choices affecting the environment (and all choices do) and think critically about ethical solutions, they are ethicating.[22]

The "Ethicating" Process

The ethicating process begins when one is presented with a problem to solve that involves making an ethical choice among various courses of action. The process proceeds through the following steps:

1. select accurate and relevant facts (information);

2. create or select knowledge relative to the problem;

3. use that knowledge to decide what should be done, why it should be done, how it should be done, and when it should be done;

4. filter this knowledge through personal and societal beliefs, attitudes, values, and prioritizing principles;

5. make a decision whether or not to act—an ethical choice.

Some people may be concerned that teachers will advocate primarily human-centered values; others may worry that teachers will advocate Earth-centered values. Teachers who provide a safe learning community, regardless of their worldviews on nature, can allow diverse beliefs, attitudes, and values to be expressed.

The action learning component of values education has caused considerable controversy. Critics assert that community action translates to student activism, which is considered an inappropriate role for public education. Yet, people often criticize students for being uninterested in politics and community issues. Proponents assert that action learning translates into responsible citizenship, which they consider a desirable educational goal in a democracy. How can the action component mean such radically different things to different people? This conflict must be resolved before a teacher can feel confident about helping students develop an environmental ethic.

In their book *Environmental Problem Solving*, Lisa A. Bardwell, Martha C. Monroe, and Margaret T. Tudor analyze four models for acting on environmental values. The authors name each model after its major spokesperson: Harold Hungerford, William F. Hammond, Bill Stapp, or Ian Robottom. Each model aims to empower learners to solve problems in their own communities and enables students to get out of the indoor classroom and become involved in the outdoor classroom. The designers of all four approaches hope to prepare students for a lifetime of community involvement in democratic and civic actions. They urge careful investigation of local problems and pursuit of those issues that have meaning and relevance to students. They agree on the value of interdisciplinary approaches to problem solving. They also recognize the importance of teacher education programs in preparing educators for this difficult and rewarding task.

However, the four models differ about the best way to implement action. Each makes different assumptions about teaching and learning. Their developers differ about the amount of structure to provide students, whether or not to teach needed investigation skills before the local action begins, and the role the teacher plays in the process. Hungerford's model provides the most structure in systematically progressing through an issue-investigation process, employing scientific methods and logical approaches to decision making and problem solution. Robottom advocates a more open-ended approach to action learning in which the investigation lends more influence to the unfolding structure and direction of the actions. Stapp's and Hammond's approaches assume middle-ground positions. These differences are to be expected because they reflect different educational philosophies. Diverse philosophies also exist among educators. Even though it is tempting to recommend one type of action approach over another, in reality, educators will use models that fit their students and their communities—both philosophically and in terms of desired competencies.[23]

What the Critics Say

A small group of vocal critics opposes student involvement in environmental action learning in the public school setting. The primary role of public educators, according to these observers, is to provide accurate and reliable knowledge to students about the environment, but to avoid the action component. They oppose students trying to solve problems related to human interactions with nature and also oppose introducing strong opinions about the role humans play in preserving or degrading the environment. This group is less convinced or denies that humans are to blame for changes in nature such as global warming. They often object to nonhuman interests being placed on an equal level with human interests in decision-making situations. For many of these critics, economic values rank high, and if a conflict exists between preserving jobs for humans and preserving a form of nonhuman nature, human jobs usually prevail.

In *Are We Building Environmental Literacy: A Report by the Independent Commission on Environmental Education*, the commission notes the lack of consensus on the meaning of *environmentally responsible behavior*. They are concerned with the inadequate treatment of scientific information, economics, and risk analysis in upper-level instructional materials. Based on a content evaluation of selected K-12 teaching resources, the commission made several recommendations:

- The primary emphasis should be placed on the acquisition of knowledge.
- Lower elementary students should begin the study of science with the natural world.
- Environmental education should be taught as an upper-level, multidisciplinary capstone course so that students can integrate knowledge from the disciplines learned at lower levels.
- Professional scientific and educational organizations should recommend educational materials after substantive review.
- Environmental science textbook publishers should evaluate their peer review process.
- Scientists, economists, and other experts, along with parents and teachers, should select environmental education materials at state and local levels.
- Teachers need substantive preparation in science, economics, and mathematics to teach environmental education.[24]

The commission strongly advocates using the outdoors for instruction and engendering a stewardship ethic in children as appropriate goals for education. However, it expresses concern for "advocacy creeping into K-12 curriculum," "brainwashed" children, and creating ecoactivists.[25]

The commission recognizes the role of the school in promoting good behavior toward humans and nature, but does not believe schools should promote a particular point of view, encourage political advocacy, or permit environmental activism by students. The report also states teachers should challenge students to think critically about controversial environmental issues. The report does not explain how a stewardship ethic can be engendered without building nature advocacy, critical thinking, and ecoactivism components into the curriculum.

What would happen if a group of students, after extensive study of an issue, wanted to write letters to the city council or speak at a public meeting to criticize a decision to develop the last woodlot in town? Would the students' decision (arrived at after analyzing and thinking critically about the facts) to become involved (advocacy based on their stewardship ethic) be considered ecoactivism or a civic responsibility? The commission needs to address these questions if it intends to influence educational practice.

In summary, critics charge that contemporary environmental instruction tends to contain factual errors and omissions, provide inadequate grounding in science and economics, encourage student pessimism and alarmist reactions, and emphasize political advocacy and action at the expense of knowledge and understanding.[26]

Instructional Challenges

Teaching environmental values and ethics presents several challenges. Kirschenbaum suggests "the goal of teaching ethics is to get each student to internalize a set of ethical filters . . . to be used to evaluate ethical issues that arise."[27]

Educators need to develop and continue to refine a set of principles to help them make difficult ethical choices. Students should be encouraged to ask questions such as these:

- Would I want the same solution applied to me if roles were reversed? (principle of reciprocity) Could I accept a fine for highway littering without thinking of it as unfair?

- Would I want everyone in the world to employ this solution or follow this example? (principle of universality) Is it acceptable for every adult in the world to drive a car that gets low gas mileage?

- Is the rule applied similarly to other individuals or groups? (principle of equity) Are toxic-waste dump sites fairly distributed among people of all social classes?

- How would I view the situation if I did not have a personal interest in it? (principle of neutrality) Even though I live in a rural area, should I be concerned about preserving open space in metropolitan areas?

- What solution would be best for the greatest number? (principle of utility) Should everyone be required to recycle aluminum cans to conserve metal and energy?

These five filters or principles can be used to examine each ethical issue as it arises. For example, when contemplating whether or not to pick a certain plant, apply principles of reciprocity, universality, equity, neutrality, and utility to see if they influence the final decision one way or the other.

In their article "Are We Ready for Ecological Commandments?" Paul A. Yambert and Carolyn F. Donow offer suggestions for overcoming three problems of teaching environmental ethics. The first problem stems from the isolation of academic disciplines and the resulting difficulties philosophers, psychologists, and ecologists have in communicating with one another. The authors suggest that everyone should take more liberal arts courses and that interdisciplinary research teams should investigate environmental issues. This strategy is described as the *two cultures solution*, that is, bringing together the sciences and humanities to study environmental issues, and deciding how to change people's behaviors.

The second problem centers on how the human brain processes and uses information and the degree of complexity it can handle. Yambert and Donow raise questions about the human capacity to demonstrate concern for other people and species, now and in the future. They wonder if the human brain can fully understand the ramifications of our interactions with the Earth. The solution is to provide an educational program that stresses nature's and human nature's multiple interrelationships so students emerge with a community view of Earth. This broader view helps students see problems and processes more universally and less egotistically.

The third problem deals with how humans view their role in the rest of nature. Yambert and Donow suggest the "Neanderthal problem" is a survival mentality of conquest over nature, which arose long ago. They contend that since our ethical systems originated long before we knew much about ecology, ethical and ecological thinking are not compatible. The solution to this problem lies again in education. The challenge is to change some basic assumptions about our place on Earth. One way of accomplishing this is to teach students by modeling Earth-centered behaviors. This requires a set of ecological rules or principles to guide human behavior. Devising a set of rules as a group project with your students would be a powerful way to learn about constructing an environmental ethic.[28]

Acting on our values is difficult because we usually hold a variety of conflicting values and sometimes they all seem important. We say we want to prevent as much pollution as possible, but we continue to drive cars. We say that we want natural cycles to continue under healthy conditions and that we should follow the laws of nature, but we tolerate pesticides and other toxic chemicals on our fruits and vegetables.

To live in our "advanced" society, we often find that our ecological values conflict with economic, safety, sanitation, convenience, comfort, pleasure, aesthetic, or educational values. How can we live our lives and reach the right balance between our needs and the needs of nature? For example, it usually costs the consumer more money (economic value) to use recycled paper and other products to conserve trees. Using a child's safety car seat (safety value) contaminates the Earth by adding industrial pollution in its manufacturing process. Putting garbage in plastic bags (sanitation value) prevents flies from reproducing but uses some of the Earth's nonrenewable materials. Heating the house in cold weather to keep warm (comfort value) affects the temperature of the atmosphere and uses up fuel.

Our modern lifestyles invite daily conflicts of values and ethical dilemmas. We cannot live without consuming the Earth's gifts and as a consequence polluting its air, water, and soil. All we can really do is to make informed choices about behaviors that have less impact. One difficult challenge is to find the information needed to make better decisions. Another challenge is to disregard the media blitz that urges us to buy products designed to make our lives better or easier.

Making students aware of these conflicting values helps them realize that various options exist for setting priorities in one situation versus another. To do this, they must identify the values—and the sources of those values—at work in each situation. When I drive to work instead of walk, I may be putting convenience or health values over ecological ones. However, when I buy a car that gets 40 miles to the gallon instead of one that gets 20, I may be putting ecological values over economic or comfort ones. Being able to separate our vital needs from our wants and desires is a useful exercise essential for assuring a sustainable Earth. Awareness of which value is taking priority in each instance can help us develop our environmental ethic.

Assessing the Development of an Environmental Ethic

Accumulating knowledge about teaching and learning is a continuous process. As new information emerges about how the brain functions, we are learning more about assessment. One meaning of the word assessment is to "assist the judge." The more ways we find to assist the judge, the better. Students, teachers, and the community should all serve as judges of an environmental ethic.

Educators use the terms *authentic* or *alternative assessment* to describe a broader view of making judgments about work quality. Recent literature has introduced the idea of portfolios, or records of students' best work. Sometimes this takes the form of exhibitions and public presentations. A comprehensive assessment program is composed of three kinds of evidence: (1) observations of behaviors and student interviews, (2) work projects and products, and (3) teacher-made and other types of tests.

Teachers can record various indicators of student learning by following a detailed program of authentic assessment. These indica-

Some Big Ideas about Educating for Environmental Ethics

Here are some thoughts for teachers engaged in helping others develop their environmental ethics:

- Maintain hope and optimism that we can make a positive difference in changing how students relate to and improve the natural world.

- Deal with controversial issues and problems with fairness and respect for the various environmental worldviews held by others and obtain administrative support for dealing with controversy in the classroom.

- Create a safe, caring, and democratic learning community to enable students to share their beliefs, attitudes, values, principles, and feelings openly and honestly.

- Select appropriate values education teaching strategies for students functioning at different levels of intellectual, social, and moral development.

- Use the community and surrounding areas as an expanded classroom in which students directly investigate natural and cultural environments.

- Identify and study the lives of environmental heroes, heroines, and mentors who have contributed to improving the quality of the natural world.

- Recognize that choices and decisions about how to use the natural world properly are made by considering cognitive, emotional, spiritual, and physical components of human nature.

- Model a personal lifestyle that reflects an environmental ethic and help students examine their own lifestyles and their impacts on the natural world.

- Consider appropriate curriculum content that minimizes the possibility of creating fear and apathy in students.

- Recognize that environmental issues and problems are usually complex, meaning that simple decisions and solutions are often incomplete.

- Realize that living in complete harmony with one's environmental ethic is rarely possible, but that does not mean these ideals should be abandoned.

- Know that humanity may never fully understand its impact on ecosystems and that science alone cannot dictate how humans should behave.
- Define key terms such as nature, environment, stewardship, natural resources, crisis, responsible action, and pollution to minimize confusion about their various meanings.
- Clarify the types of environmental values the community will permit to be inculcated (instilled) and those they want students to choose for themselves (clarified) after careful consideration and critical thought.
- Encourage students to defend and justify the reasons for holding certain values, attitudes, beliefs, feelings, and principles about how they interact with the natural world.

tors can take the form of actual behaviors, both in and out of school, or expressions of interest, enthusiasm, and curiosity. Some teachers also keep track of the types of questions students ask about a topic.

One suggestion for assessing students' environmental ethic development is to ask them to write a brief statement about their associations with nature and how they perceive their responsibilities toward using and protecting it. This statement might be as short as several sentences or as long as an essay. The statement could be rewritten several times throughout the year to assess student ability to incorporate new knowledge and experiences in presenting a statement of personal ethics. Interesting comparisons of beliefs, attitudes, and values can be made by examining several statements written over time.

Over a period of a year, I have written several beliefs, attitudes, and values that make up my land ethic:

I will live with fewer material things and consume less because manufacturing processes pollute the Earth.

I will walk more lightly on the Earth by recycling as many household items as I can to conserve energy and resources.

I will consider how my lifestyle impacts the Earth's systems and make some sacrifices.

I have a deep respect for the sacredness of nature and will honor it by expressing my gratitude for its gifts.

Because I care for nature, I will make sacrifices for the long-term betterment of all.

I should learn more about educating for an environmental ethic and the negative impacts of technology on nature.

You notice I selected specific things I believe are right and other things that are wrong. I also considered my relationship to nature, technology, and my community, both now and in the future. Underlying these statements is knowledge about how nature works and how my lifestyle relates to nature. As we develop and refine our knowledge base, we usually identify certain indicators of understanding. These indicators lead to and result from belief, attitude, and value changes and determine how we will interact with nature.

These indicators of understanding could be used in assessing student growth in developing an environmental ethic. Perhaps you and your students could add more indicators as your experience and knowledge expands.

This chapter has outlined a brief history of values education and provided some suggestions for recognizing and assessing student growth in developing an environmental ethic. In the next chapter, we examine specific activities designed to help in the process.[29]

Indicators of Understanding an Environmental Ethic

Persons who are developing their environmental ethic will demonstrate a willingness to take these actions:

- Consider long-range environmental impacts of human actions as well as short-range impacts.
- Consider the implications of human actions from national and global perspectives, as well as from local and regional perspectives.
- Consider whether or not to use fewer materials from nature because of the potential harm to nature's cycles and systems.
- Intervene in certain natural cycles in ways that respect what we know about how these systems work.
- Forego certain pleasures, comforts, conveniences, and short-term economic advantages to preserve nonhuman organisms, energy, and ecosystems.
- Support certain low-impact activities that promote the care of the land with time and money.
- Learn about individuals and cultures that have modeled environmental concern and action, and adopt some of these values and behaviors.
- Keep informed about specific land issues and problems and their possible solutions.
- View land decisions as ethical acts based on principles of what is right and good to do.
- Become involved in educational, political, or legal activities to promote concern for nature.
- View nature as a model with the potential to teach us how to live healthy lifestyles.
- Adopt values of respect, gratitude, compassion, caring, reverence, and empathy for nature.
- Develop feelings of humility toward our role in nature and view the needs of nature as equal in worth to the needs of humans in some situations.
- Develop skills leading to ecological and societal understandings of a particular geographical place or bioregion.
- Expand the concept of *community* beyond humans to include entire ecosystems and their components.
- Display the courage, curiosity, and conviction to serve as an advocate for preserving and protecting nature.
- Examine critically the interactions of technology and lifestyle choices and determine their impacts on nature.

Notes

[1] Thomas Lickona, *Educating for Character: How Our Schools Can Teach Respect and Responsibility* (New York: Bantam, 1991), 38.

[2] Timothy Beatley, *Ethical Land Use: Principles of Policy and Planning* (Baltimore: Johns Hopkins University Press, 1994), 30.

[3] Carl R. Rogers, "Toward a Modern Approach to Values: The Valuing Process in the Mature Person," in *Readings in Values Clarification*, comp. Sidney B. Simon and Howard Kirschenbaum (Minneapolis: Winston Press, 1973), 77.

[4] *Merriam-Webster's Collegiate Dictionary*, 10th ed. (Springfield, MA: Merriam-Webster, 1996), 756.

[5] Kempton, Boster, and Hartley, *Environmental Values in American Culture*, 12; Michael J. Caduto, *A Guide on Environmental Values Education* (Paris: UNESCO, 1985), 7. Caduto's book is available from the author, P.O. Box 1052, Norwich, VT 05055, telephone 802-649-1815.

[6] Michael S. Spranger, "Global Environmental Values and Ethics: A Challenge for Educators" (paper presented at National Science Foundation Middle School Teacher Training Workshop, Biloxi, MS, 18 June 1993), 7-8.

[7] Howard Kirschenbaum, *100 Ways to Enhance Values and Morality in Schools and Youth Settings* (Boston: Allyn and Bacon, 1995), 14.

[8] Ibid., 15-28.

[9] Kevin Ryan, "The New Moral Education," *Phi Delta Kappan* 68 (November 1986): 228-33.

[10] Caduto, *Guide on Environmental Values Education*, 19.

[11] To read more about inculcation, see Lickona, *Educating for Character*.

[12] For more information about this strategy, read Louis E. Raths, Merrill Harmin, and Sidney B. Simon, *Values and Teaching: Working with Values in the Classroom*, 2d ed. (Columbus, OH: C. E. Merrill Publishing Company, 1978).

[13] For more information about analyzing environmental issues, read Harold Hungerford, R. Ben Peyton, John Ramsey, and Trudi L. Volk, *Investigating and Evaluating Environmental Issues and Actions: Skill Development Modules* (Champaign, IL: Stipes Publishing L.L.C., 1992).

[14] For more information about this approach, read Reimer, Paolitto, and Hersh, *Promoting Moral Growth*; Jean Piaget, *The Child's Conception of the World* (1929; reprint, Paterson, NJ: Littlefield, Adams, 1963); Piaget, *The Origins of Intelligence in Children* (New York: International Universities Press, 1952); Piaget, *Six Psychological Studies* (New York: Random House, 1967); Kohlberg, "Continuities in Childhood and Adult Moral Development Revisited"; and Kohlberg, "Stages of Moral Development as a Basis for Moral Education."

[15] For further information, read Rahima C. Wade, ed., *Community Service-Learning: A Guide to Including Service in the Public School Curriculum* (Albany: State University of New York Press, 1997).

[16] For more information on confluent outdoor learning, read Joseph Cornell, *Listening to Nature: How to Deepen Your Awareness of Nature* (Nevada City, CA: Dawn Publications, 1987).

[17] Matthews and Riley, *Teaching and Evaluating Outdoor Ethics*, iii-v, 8.

[18] Lickona, *Educating for Character*, 28-30.

[19] Ibid., 29.

[20] For a comprehensive treatment of this study, see Harold R. Hungerford, William J. Bluhm, Trudi L. Volk, and John Ramsey, *Essential Readings in Environmental Education* (Champaign, IL: Stipes Publishing L.L.C., 1998).

[21] Alan Guebert, "AG Biotech: Just Because We Can?" *CountryView*, 31 March 1998, 8.

[22] Milton McClaren, letter to author, January 1998.

[23] Lisa A. Bardwell, Martha C. Monroe, and Margaret T. Tudor, *Environmental Problem Solving: Theory, Practice and Possibilities in Environmental Education* (Troy, OH: North American Association for Environmental Education, 1994), 21-84.

[24] Independent Commission on Environmental Education, *Are We Building Environmental Literacy? A Report by the Independent Commission on Environmental Education* (Washington, DC: George C. Marshall Institute, 1997), 2-4.

[25] Ibid., 5-6.

[26] Kelly V. Glenn, ed., *The Free Market Environmental Bibliography*, 4th ed. (Washington, DC: Competitive Enterprise Institute, 1996), 99.

[27] Kirschenbaum, *100 Ways to Enhance Values*, 121-22.

[28] Paul A. Yambert and Carolyn F. Donow, "Are We Ready for Ecological Commandments?" *Journal of Environmental Education* 17 (summer 1986): 13-16.

[29] For historical background and case study examples of teaching for values formation and valuing skills development, see William Ayers, Jean Ann Hunt, and Therese Quinn, eds., *Teaching for Social Justice: A* Democracy and Education *Reader* (New York: New Press and Teachers College Press, 1998) and Melinda Fine, *Habits of the Mind: Struggling over Values in America's Classrooms* (San Francisco: Jossey-Bass, 1995).

CHAPTER 5

What Activities Can Teachers Use to Help Students Develop an Environmental Ethic?

All studies arise from aspects of the one earth and the one life lived upon it. We do not have a series of stratified earths, one of which is mathematical, another physical, another historical, and so on.

—John Dewey, *The School and Society*

I am trying to teach you that this alphabet of 'natural objects' (soils and rivers, birds and beasts) spells out a story. . . . Once you learn to read the land I have no fear of what you will do to it, or with it.

—Aldo Leopold, *The River of the Mother of God and Other Essays*

Designing Environmental Values and Ethics Activities

John Dewey's and Aldo Leopold's words have particular meaning for those concerned with using various instructional methods to help students develop an environmental ethic. Most of the knowledge in the world originates from the Earth and how humans interact with it.

This knowledge can be used either to help the Earth continue to function in healthy ways or to use the Earth in ways that slowly degrades it. This chapter categorizes some of the knowledge about developing an environmental ethic according to various instructional methods, not the traditional subject matter areas. Educators will certainly recognize familiar subject matter such as math, science, language arts, and history. In developing an environmental ethic, scholars draw from a wide array of disciplines. Experienced teachers will be able to use activities from this chapter appropriately in educational programs that deliver traditional subject matter. Lessons may be integrated into an existing curriculum or combined to create a special unit.

Leopold was convinced that once people learned to read the alphabet of nature (the soils, rivers, birds, beasts, and so forth), they would eventually know how to live in harmony with the Earth. If they learned this lesson well, he had no fear about what they would do to it or with it. Numerous examples can be found of people who know this alphabet intimately and live in ways that carefully consider their impact on nature. Leopold was a strong believer in outdoor experience as a way to learn about our connections to the Earth. Sometimes he taught in the field and also did much of his research there. He knew how to read the land and share that language with others. Direct experience outside the classroom is important, but students need to apply critical thinking to the process.

These activities focus mainly on values and ethics related to Earth-centered worldviews. They encourage educational experiences outside the classroom and in the community, and they ask students to reflect on these experiences. They include nonhuman and human nature as topics to be studied. The format for most of the activities includes (1) a set of directions for what to do and how to do it, (2) opportunities to do the activity, (3) a coming together with others to analyze and share the results, and (4) opportunities to discuss the meanings and applications of these events in the lives of students. This four-part sequence is known as the experiential learning cycle, a very old model that is still important for today's youth. The experiences emphasize direct contacts with the natural and built environments studied in the context of a local area. Pencils, paper, hand lenses, and other simple materials will allow the senses to be engaged and expanded and will help in the learning process. Teachers can help students internalize ethics-based experiences by leading reflection sessions that direct student thinking toward integrating and applying them.

This chapter suggests activities that encourage students to think critically about some of their beliefs, attitudes, and values. The existing bias of the selected activities leans toward the Earth-centered end of the continuum; the author's premise is that members of modern society are already all-too-well versed in the human-centered view. There are literally thousands of activities available in the education literature, but few authors have organized them according to instructional methods or focused them sharply on values and ethics. The activities are drawn from my reading and teaching experiences spanning kindergarten to graduate school over more than 37 years. Activities that can be traced to a particular source are referenced in the notes. Feel free to modify and adapt the activities to fit your student level, geographic area, and teaching objectives and style.

The 40 activities fall into 11 categories:

- Thinking and Discussion (1-4)
- Solo Reflection (5-7)
- Writing to Connect (8-10)
- Nature Observances and Ceremonies (11-13)
- Questioning (14-16)
- Codes of Ethics (17-19)
- Heroes, Heroines, and Mentors (20-21)
- Action Projects (22-23)
- Creating Beauty (24-26)
- Literature Springboards (27-36)
- Games and Simulations (37-40)

Thinking and Discussion

Let's begin our adventure into the alphabet of nature to develop literacy in environmental ethics. The opening activities, "Taking Stock," "Environmental Ethics Quiz," "Environmental Ethics Issues in the Newspaper," and "Minus, Zero, and Plus Ethics," give the students something to think about and discuss. By assuming listening and questioning roles, educators can understand students' beliefs, attitudes, values, principles, and past experiences related to these topics. With this information, future lessons can be planned more effectively.

Activity 1. Taking Stock: What Does Nature and Environment Mean?

Encouraging students to talk about their relationship with nature and the environment can bring to light some of their environmental values and ethics. Communicating about these topics can also unearth hidden assumptions, biases, and confusion about humanity's role as an ecological citizen. After filling out this questionnaire or discussing the items in small groups, have students explain and defend their responses.

1. When you hear the words *nature* and *environment*, do you picture humans as being part of this picture?

2. Do you consider nature and human nature to be two separate things?

3. Is nature something mostly to cooperate with or something to try to control?

4. Do you seek out nature programs on TV or in the theater? Why or why not? On the average, how much time do you spend watching nature shows each month?

5. If you were seeking a place to find peace and relaxation, would you go indoors or outdoors? What would you do there?

6. In your free time, do you like to participate in outdoor recreation such as boating, hiking, or bird watching? Why or why

not? What is the impact of these activities on the quality of the environment?

7. Buckminster Fuller, an inventor and philosopher, once said: "The environment is everything except me." Do you agree with his definition? Can you offer a better one?

8. The word *natural* has many meanings and is sometimes used to sell things. Do you tend to buy natural products? Why or why not? Give examples.

9. What kinds of nature can you find in the city? In the country? In the suburbs? Where can you find more nature?

10. Is nature more a scary thing or a comforting thing? Give examples.

11. How do different technologies separate you from nature? Join you more closely to nature?

12. If the word *environment* means both natural and human-made things, doesn't it become a meaningless term because it includes everything?

13. What parts of nature do you like to include as decorations in your room and home? Why are you attracted to these things?

14. How have words from nature been used to name sports teams, cars, streets, clothing, cities, and other aspects of our culture?

15. Do some human cultures seem to honor and respect nature more than others? Give examples.

16. Make a list of rules for how your classmates should use nature and behave in natural areas. What are the three most important rules to include?

17. If humans are a part of nature (human nature), does that mean all of their inventions (technologies) are natural? Explain your position.

18. Do you have other questions about nature and environment? Make a list.

Activity 2. Environmental Ethics Quiz

Directions: Answer the following questions with a yes, no, or maybe. Be prepared to defend your answers.

Would you . . .

1. remove English sparrow eggs from a nesting box so bluebirds could nest there?

2. remove exotic garlic mustard plants from the forest to help native wildflowers grow better?

3. assist the city council in drafting an ordinance to eliminate weeds (unwanted plants) such as ragweed from growing within the city limits?

4. favor controlling populations of coyotes because they occasionally attack pet dogs?

5. help others erect squirrel-proof bird feeders to prevent squirrels from reaching the seeds?

6. favor trapping wild turkeys and Canada geese and removing them from places where they bother people?

7. ask a taxidermist to mount a large trophy fish you caught for a nature center display?

8. attempt to attract an owl by using a tape-recorded owl call at night so you can teach others about owl behavior?

9. pick a dandelion flower so you can give everyone in the group a floret to examine?

10. dig up and cut a bloodroot plant to teach others about the poisonous, blood-like sap in the rootstock?

11. remove a Solomon's seal plant from the ground to show the seal-like markings on the root?

12. cut down a basswood tree sapling to make cordage from the inner bark for constructing a display wigwam?

13. photograph a hummingbird's nest filled with young to add to your educational slide collection, even if it frightens the birds?

14. cut evergreen branches and ferns for a centerpiece to decorate a banquet table?

15. gather Queen Anne's lace flowers for a floral arrangement in your home?

16. cut living hickory tree branches to get sticks for roasting marshmallows at a campfire?

17. fish for trout with worms and a barbed hook even though you know some fish will probably swallow the hook and die?

18. buy and wear clothing made from wild animal skins or fur?

19. walk alongside a muddy and slippery forest trail even if you know you are widening it and causing erosion?

20. remove hanging grapevines from forest trees near a park so children will not be tempted to swing and injure themselves?

21. remove a patch of poison ivy from an outdoor study area to protect young children who might walk there?

22. set a spring trap to catch a mouse found eating food in your kitchen?

23. slap and kill a mosquito on your arm before it bites you?

24. dig a deep trench around a tent pitched in the forest to prevent rain from flowing under the tent?

25. attend a rodeo or circus for entertainment?

26. cut blue jay feathers into small pieces to demonstrate how they look even if you know it is against the law to possess a songbird feather?

27. keep a flint spear point found along the trail in a state park even though you know that taking things from the park is forbidden?

28. transplant a lady's slipper orchid from someone's private land to your backyard wildflower garden even though it might die?

29. hike on land marked with a "no trespassing" sign without obtaining the owner's permission?

30. use an eagle feather found outside a zoo cage to make a Native American dreamcatcher even though possessing an eagle feather is illegal if you are not a Native American?

31. bury food waste from a picnic in a deep hole in the forest even though you know it will take a long time to decay?

Activity 3. Environmental Ethics Issues in the Newspaper

Newspapers are steady sources of information about issues affecting the quality of the environment. Humans continuously face decisions about how their lifestyles impact ecosystems and natural cycles. The following questions can help students learn more about environmental ethics from the newspaper.

1. Examine articles that deal with pollution. What types of pollution disturb you the most? The least? Explain why.

2. Can you detect any biases journalists may have about how humans should behave toward the environment? What evidence can you find to support your claims?

3. Judging from the types of articles published in the newspaper, can you determine whether the editors have a bias toward human use of natural areas or preservation of natural areas?

4. What generalizations can you make about the predominant worldview of our society from analyzing newspaper content?

5. What evidence can you find that nature is viewed as humanity's *enemy*? As humanity's *friend*?

6. Can you categorize environmental issues into similar groupings and then draw generalizations about these issues?

7. Find editorials, cartoons, and letters to the editor that you agree with and that you disagree with. Have you ever written an editorial or letter to the editor about an environmental issue? Why or why not?

8. Select an article, cartoon, or letter that describes an environmental issue. Identify the following: the major issue, the conflicting parties, some of the values held by the different parties, and the environmental ethics views or positions held by the different parties.

9. What can you tell about the worldview of a newspaper's editors from the types of articles that do *not* appear?

Activity 4. Minus, Zero, and Plus Ethics

In *The First Book of Ethics*, Algernon D. Black described three approaches to ethics—*minus, zero,* and *plus*.[1] *Minus Ethics* involves warning others that they should not do certain things but does not involve taking any other personal action. Such warnings could be called "you shall not" commandments:

- don't be a litterbug
- don't carve your initials in trees
- don't buy overpackaged products

Zero Ethics is a neutral approach that defines *being good* as the same as *not doing bad.* Individuals subscribing to this approach might practice the following behaviors but be reluctant to urge others to emulate their example:

- not littering
- not carving initials in trees
- not buying overpackaged products

Plus Ethics involves taking positive actions to benefit people or the environment:

- cleaning up a littered highway
- making a poster to persuade people not to carve initials in trees
- writing the manufacturer of an overpackaged product to convey disapproval

Have students examine their behaviors related to the environment and make a list identifying their *minus, zero,* and *plus* environmental ethics. Then, ask them the following reflection questions:

- Was it easier to make some lists than others? Why?
- Was one list longer than the other two? What does that indicate to you about yourself?
- Are there any actions that appear on all three lists? What does that indicate to you about yourself?
- Did you discover any new ethical actions you would like to adopt into your lifestyle? If so, which ones?

Solo Reflection

Spending time alone allows opportunities to connect with the Earth and can contribute to values formation. Beginning in early childhood, children form nature values and ethics by spending time outdoors away from other people under favorable conditions. These activities provide some structure to help students get the most from this solitude.

Activity 5. Images of Nature

There are many meanings for the word *nature*. Allow students to find examples of various ways of viewing nature by using quotations to stimulate and guide their thoughts. The following quotes illustrate a variety of views of nature; ask students to name an example of each.

- **Wisdom:** "Never does Nature say one thing and wisdom another." (Juvenal)
- **Healer:** "I firmly believe that nature brings solace in all troubles." (Anne Frank)
- **Separated from humans:** "How can we reenter the first world of nature, from which we have alienated ourselves?" (Loren Eiseley)
- **Human:** "All who achieve greatness in art . . . possess one thing in common: they are one with nature." (Basho)
- **Feminine:** "We cannot command nature except by obeying her." (Francis Bacon)
- **Teacher:** "Come forth into the light of things. Let nature be your teacher." (William Wordsworth)

Invite students to find other images of nature—for example, as something to control, as a creative force, or as it connects to all life. Are some images easier to find? Which ones?[2]

Activity 6. Giving Yourself a Present

We spend much of our time thinking about the past and future. This focus can be helpful at times; however, we sometimes miss most of what is going on in the present. Imagine gathering your past and future in a large box. Take a few minutes to do this and close the lid tightly. Then take the box and bury it for the moment. You can always dig it up later. Now you can fully concentrate on the present to do the following:

1. Look at plants and try to see signs of them growing.

2. If a drop of water is available, try to see if it is evaporating.

3. Locate an animal, even if it is small. What can you learn by observing it carefully?

4. Look at an object and trace its shape with your eyes. Did this help you notice details that you might have missed before?

5. Use your senses of touch, hearing, and smell. Try using them separately and then in different combinations.

Was it difficult to keep your awareness focused on the present? Why or why not? Which senses are best for use with distant objects? For use with close objects?[3]

Activity 7. Nature's Jigsaw

The Earth's components are like pieces of a giant jigsaw puzzle that form a picture of life. Sit quietly and select an object representing one piece of the puzzle, such as a rock or a bird. Try to find evidence of how that object connects to others in the puzzle. Evaluate how these connections support life and how they harm life. Be sure to support your judgments with reasons. What would the picture look like if some of the puzzle pieces were lost? Is it right to allow puzzle pieces to disappear through pollution? Are there some puzzle pieces that could be lost without much impact on the whole ecosystem picture?

Try diagraming the links in the product chains:

my book ➡ paper ➡ pulp ➡ tree

ink ➡ dyes ➡ iron, cobalt copper, carbon

binding thread ➡ cotton ➡ cotton plant

What else is needed to make these chains work
(energy, machines, etc.)?

Writing to Connect

Writing can connect students with the surrounding world. It is a way to capture and record impressions for later examination. Give students pencils and paper, and ask them to observe and record their impressions. Taking field notes and recording entries in journals over time provides rich information for identifying personal beliefs, attitudes, and values about nature.

Activity 8. Chain Links

When humans convert nature into useful products, the manufacturing process involves various steps along a chain of events. The Chain Links activity allows students to trace a part of nature as it is converted into items useful to humans. It also helps trace manufactured products back to their sources in nature.

For example, find a tree and list the steps needed to convert a tree into a wooden table, or find a wooden table and trace the steps back to a tree. Next, find a sidewalk and list the steps involved in taking it back to its limestone source in the ground, or reverse the process and take the limestone through the steps to create concrete.

Sit quietly in different natural and urban places to make lists. Think about common objects used every day and where they come from. What is the role of technology in this process?

How would knowing some of these links affect how you value nature? Technology? Are you willing to pay more for something if you know producing it harms natural systems less than producing it another way?

What information is missing from what you can observe in nature? How can you get this missing information?

Activity 9. Walking Gently on the Earth

We cannot live without making an impact on Earth. However, our choices determine if we walk gently or violently. With every breath, we add carbon dioxide to the air. With every step in the forest, we compact the soil. Wearing clothes means something has been taken from nature at a cost to the Earth. Take a walk outside and record the ways you impact the Earth. All life has environmental consequences.

How do you distinguish between proper use (which gives something back) and consumption (which uses but does not give back)?

Write a story about someone who walks gently on the Earth and someone else who walks violently on the Earth. In fact, we all do both, but for some, the balance is tipped one way or the other. Read the finished stories to others and discuss the different impressions of gentle and violent living.

How could you live more gently?

Design a *green* school or other building that makes a minimal impact on the Earth, both in its construction and operation.

Does the word *progress* mean the same thing to everyone?

The U.S. government requires an environmental impact statement to be written before humans can change nature through development. Visit a natural area and predict the impact of a dam, a road, a shopping mall, or an amusement park. Visit a developed area, or one being developed, and ask how it is being changed by human acts. Are these changes good or bad? For whom? How do we decide?[4]

Activity 10. Keeping Tabs on the Season

During the springtime, write journal entries recording when different plants emerge from the ground, sprout leaves, and flower. Also record when migrating animals return.

During the fall, write journal entries recording when different leaves begin to turn color or fall from the plants, or when different animals leave.

Write about your beliefs, attitudes, and values associated with each season. Do you appreciate one season over another? Share your reasons for choosing a favorite season.

You may want to compare the information about when these events happen each year to see if spring and fall occur earlier or later. Aldo Leopold's descendants have found that spring flowers bloom about two weeks later now than when Leopold kept his journal in the 1930s and 1940s. Does this tell us something about global warming? What could it mean in regard to changing our lifestyles? This question has created lots of newspaper copy and discussions.

How does one prove that certain human activities are changing the Earth?

Nature Observances and Ceremonies

People have engaged in many nature observances and ceremonies for thousands of years. This is one way to express gratitude for the gifts of nature. You can invent your own observances and ceremonies and share them with your group. First, become aware of natural processes such as seeds sprouting, wind blowing, plants growing, or logs decaying. The word *ceremony* comes from the Latin meaning sacredness, so be sure to select a process in nature that you respect. Students can use readings, songs, music and rhythm instruments, skits, role playing, or other forms of creative group participation. Investigate how different cultures celebrate seasonal changes and other natural events, now and in the past.

Activity 11. Appreciating an Object

First, explore the area to find something that you would like to honor. This can be a tree, rock, river, or any other natural object. Decide what is unique or special about the object you select. Plan your observances or ceremonies so others become aware of what you value most about that object. It might be its beauty, strength, graceful movements, texture, silhouette, or any other physical feature. Make sure your plan includes a group of people making direct contact with the chosen object. Now celebrate together.

Even in suburban and urban areas, students can select house plants, trees, lawns, building cornerstones, grave markers, pets, and many other evidence of nature.

How are values created and shaped by these activities?[5]

Activity 12. Mask Making

This role-playing activity is based on part of a ceremony known as a Council of All Beings. This council is described in John Seed, Joanna Macy, Pat Fleming, and Arne Naess' *Thinking Like a Mountain*. One part of the ceremony involves each member of the group representing a part of nature. Participants can choose any animal, rock, stream, mountain, or other component. Then they construct masks that represent these phenomena. When possible, the masks should contain parts of the natural objects themselves such as grass, bark, or seeds.

After the masks are constructed, the students place them over their faces and *become* their object. They do this by speaking for that object. They should try to empathize with the object and speak to the humans who sit in the center of the council ring. Throughout the council, participants take turns becoming humans again by taking off their masks and sitting silently. The point is not to have a dialogue between humans and nature, but for humans simply to listen to what nature has to say. This is based on the idea that nature may have a lot to teach humans about how their behaviors affect the Earth. Before conducting this ceremony, help students rehearse some of the things they might say in their roles. Students may wish to prepare by studying about their selected part beforehand.

Do not allow the ceremony to become too depressing. If it does, shift the discussion toward some of the positive things humans do for nature. The goal is to achieve a more balanced view of the various roles humans play on Earth and to demonstrate how human values can change. Did listening to nature *talking* affect your values? How?

A follow-up activity is to look at some actual primal masks (e.g., Northwest American Indian, African, Asian). Many cultures make rich use of masks as expressions of their worldviews. Many masks represent elements of nature, human-nature, or human-human interactions. In "After Earth Day 1990 . . . What?" Milton McClaren recounts a story of the Northwest coast Native mosquito mask worn at dance ceremonies by children. The early people were sitting around their campfire and one person suddenly grabbed a fly, throwing it into the fire. The Great Spirit was angry that the people had killed one of its creatures without thought or reason, so the Spirit caused the fire to throw off sparks. Each spark turned into a mosquito, and that is why mosquitoes were created—to remind humans to respect nature.

How do sports team and vehicle names reflect our links with nature? Does naming a team *Cardinals* reflect how we value this bird? How is nature used to sell products?

Activity 13. Symbols of Thanks

Some American Indians honor nature by giving back some special plant material such as corn meal or pollen, cedar, sage, sweet grass, or tobacco.

Find a plant part you can use to represent giving something back to the Earth in a ceremony of thanks. Before choosing a plant, figure out what makes it special for this use as a symbol of thanks and whether it is culturally appropriate to use in this way. It may be respectful to avoid traditionally sacred plants used by other cultures.

Think about what you have taken from nature recently (e.g., lettuce, carrots, rice, wheat) and then conduct a ceremony giving a piece of your special plant back to the Earth. This ceremony is especially effective when performed immediately after picking a flower, fruit, or vegetable from the garden. Students will develop a better understanding of showing reverence and reciprocity (giving back in gratitude) for the Earth gifts we enjoy. It will also help them gain greater respect for other cultures. How might our lifestyles change if we did this ceremony every day? Can ceremonies raise awareness levels of nature and influence our environmental ethic? Can our environmental ethic influence the kinds of observances and ceremonies we select?

Questioning

By asking the right questions, people can become clearer about what they value. The art and skill of asking good questions should be nurtured in students. Many educators believe asking a good question that leads to another question is just as important as asking or answering a question that results in knowledge. These activities use questions to probe topics related to the environment.

Activity 14. Creating Powerful Questions

A powerful question has at least six characteristics: (1) it leads to new questions and further discoveries; (2) it engages interest in and active involvement with a topic; (3) it helps students feel the need to know more; (4) it results in feelings of success and accomplishment; (5) it notes the importance of people, objects, events, time sequence, locations or origins, reasons, and values; and (6) it stimulates further discussions.

Ask students to go outside and find something they value. Direct them to create several powerful questions that will help others understand more about why they value that natural object or event. For example, a student who chooses a flower might ask the following questions:

- Are there any others around that look as beautiful?
- Could an artist duplicate the detail of the leaf veins?
- Has there ever been another flower that looked exactly like this one?
- Will there ever be one in the future that looks exactly like this one?
- Would you rather have this flower "live in your heart" or "die in your hand?"

Have the students lead the rest of the group to their chosen object and ask their questions. Based on responses, the group can discuss which questions they think are most powerful and why. How can values change by asking questions as well as by answering them? Is it ever ethical to pick a living flower? What principles or rules can be developed to help students sort out their beliefs, attitudes, and values? When two important values are in conflict, what rules can be applied to make the choice more ethical?

Activity 15. Picking Questions

Sometimes it is difficult to decide whether or not to pick a plant for a certain purpose. When students enter a government park or forest, there is usually a "no picking" rule in effect. Although this rule exists for good reasons, it denies students the opportunity to develop their own values about picking plants.

To help them form their own values, find a privately owned location and obtain permission to take the students there. Select a place that has plants growing in abundance. Make sure none of the plants are on the threatened or endangered lists for your area or are poisonous to the touch. Obtaining such a list from government agencies is an important step in the process of making choices.

Allow each group of students to examine one plant and to answer the following questions about it. After they have considered all the questions, ask student teams if they would pick the plant and ask them to give reasons for their decision.

1. Are there enough other plants of the same type here so we can pick one? What does "enough" mean?

2. Could we learn something important about the plant by picking it? Is learning or education high on your list of what you value?

3. Could the plant be made into a useful product (e.g., food, decoration, or tool) if we picked it? Is usefulness to humans a strong value for you?

4. Would the whole plant survive if we picked just one part of it? Is preserving all life important to you?

5. Would the area be improved by picking it? What changes are defined as improvements? As destructive acts?

6. Would the plant die soon anyway, making it permissible to pick now? How does the death of a plant affect future life in the area?

7. Is the plant safe for us to pick? What priority does the value of human safety play in your value system?

8. Would picking the plant benefit an animal or other plant in some way? Who or what should be given moral consideration?

9. Are there any other important questions to ask before we decide whether or not to pick this plant?

What will we do now? To pick or not to pick, that is the question. Of what value is this plant if we leave it where it grows? What can we learn about plant communities by studying how a plant relates to others surrounding it? What makes us believe we have the right to even consider picking this plant?

After the students make their decisions, meet in a central place to discuss their actions or nonactions. Encourage an interchange of ideas about human uses of plants. What makes it okay to pick certain plants? When is it never okay? Are some plants always okay to pick without thinking much about it? Is a plant of lesser, more, or equal value compared to animals in the pyramid of life? Do you have any plant prejudices or biases? Is it okay to have prejudices or biases toward certain plants but wrong to have prejudices and biases toward people?

Activity 16. Awareness Questions

Prepare a list of questions that will promote greater awareness of a place. Direct the students to go outside and answer as many of the questions as they can and return to a central meeting place to compare and discuss answers.

1. What is the most powerful thing here? How did you define power?

2. What is one thing missing from this place? What would you add?

3. What kinds of wastes are generated here?

4. Where is the most comfortable place to sit?

5. Where is the most beautiful place to look?

6. What is the most important living thing in this place? Nonliving thing?

7. What is the most valuable thing here? How did you measure value?

8. What is the rarest thing here?

9. Where is the most dangerous place here?

10. What is your favorite thing?

11. What is the most bothersome thing?

Codes of Ethics

A code is a statement of beliefs, attitudes, values, and principles about a particular topic. A code of ethics about the environment suggests how we should relate to nature in living as gently as possible on Earth. It should be as internally consistent as possible and offer clear and practical suggestions for making choices and guiding behavior. The code should reflect a set of statements about what is right and good to do.

Activity 17. Brainstorming "Should" Lists

This group activity is preliminary to the students writing their own environmental ethic codes.

Have them go outside individually or in groups and take notes on how humans have used and abused an area. They may select a section of park, a highway, a building site, a river, or any place as long as they can give a reasonable explanation for their choices.

Invite them inside to brainstorm a list of *shoulds* for guiding human behavior in the environment. Remember that brainstormed lists simply provide the raw materials for building their own codes at a later time. The task will be to take the brainstormed statements and decide which ones best represent their positions. After students share their lists with the rest of the group, ask whether every *should* statement represents a value.

An alternative approach is to select an area where human development exists. Ask students to respond to these questions about development in the area:

1. Should we have developed it at all? Why? Why not? Did we have alternative choices? What would have been the consequences of these other choices?

2. Given that we did develop it, what did we do right and what is considered right? Why? What did we do wrong? Why? What other options might have been considered?

Activity 18. Interviewing People in the Community

To gain more ideas for writing codes of ethics, ask students to develop an interview questionnaire about specific issues in the community. Before finalizing the questionnaire, it should be pilot tested with some residents to find out if the questions are understandable. Some researchers suggest inviting small groups of people from the community to discuss their concerns before developing the interview questions fully.

After the questionnaire has been completed, revised based on the pilot test, and agreed upon, have students interview their parents and others in the community. By compiling the results, students will get an indication of the beliefs, attitudes, and values of community members.

Here are some sample questions to ask:

1. Are humans responsible for some of the climate change in the world?

2. Do people in our community have a right to clean air? How clean must it be?

3. Would it be better to go back to the pioneer days when there was more land?

4. Should people be charged more for gasoline so that the revenues can be used to clean up the air? To build more roads?

5. Does it matter if there are no more clean streams to fish in?

6. Should we leave the Earth in better shape than we found it? If so, how?

7. Would it be a good idea to buy less so we pollute less?

Can you identify various environmental ethics that are held by various community members? Give examples.[6]

Activity 19. Codes of Behavior Developed by Special Interest Groups

People use the outdoors for many things. Recreational uses can make negative impacts on the land if human behavior is unethical. Interview different outdoor users in the community such as anglers, snowboarders, members of game and fish clubs, natural history groups, and members of four-wheel drive clubs. Ask if their groups follow special behavioral codes. Whether students realize it or not, codes are in place for photographers, nature viewers, farmers, hunters, anglers, trappers, hikers, campers, birders, and other special interest groups.

See if students can collect any of these codes by contacting the individual groups. Analyze these codes for beliefs, attitudes, values, and guiding principles. Decide which you agree with and which you do not. Do some recreational uses of the land create more impact than others? What should be done about this?

Some communities, for example, have created special management zones. They designate areas where certain uses are permitted (e.g., sports fields, hiking trails, picnicking) or restricted (e.g., no fishing, no camping, no campfires, no motors). Why have these specific codes been developed for these areas? Do you agree with them? Are people obeying them?

Heroes, Heroines, and Mentors

We develop heroes, heroines, and mentors by observing the values and actions of others. These people serve as character models for our behaviors and set standards for us to follow. We do not have to admire all the values a person holds; we can be selective.[7]

Activity 20. Identifying Characteristics

Broadly speaking, consider with the students some of the characteristics of a hero, heroine, or mentor, and apply these ideas to environmental heroes and heroines. Encourage students to find a variety of people in the community who have made the Earth a better place to live by preserving nature. The following list may help identify some relevant characteristics of these people:

1. Do they have the ability to anticipate the future (prophet)?

2. Do they search for and express what they consider to be valuable, right, and good (philosopher)?

3. Do they fight for what they consider just and fair (warrior)?

4. Do they act from a set of consistent values and principles (principled person)?

5. Do they break new ground in an area of study (pioneer)?

6. Do they take measured risks to achieve their goals (calculated risk taker)?

7. Do they clearly convey what they are thinking or feeling (communicator)?

8. Do they work hard to accomplish tasks (diligent worker)?

9. Do they seem sincere about what they are doing (genuine person)?

10. What are other questions that could be asked?

These are just some of the potential traits. Perhaps there are other characteristics students can identify and learn to admire. Challenge students to place the views of the person they talk to on the human-centered/Earth-centered continuum. The students may be interested in investigating the Greek origins of the words *hero* and *mentor*. Who in the community are good models to help you develop an environmental ethic?

Activity 21. Who Is an Environmentalist?

The label *environmentalist* means different things to different people. In a survey of American environmental values, Boster, Kempton, and Hartley found two-thirds of the people interviewed considered themselves environmentalists.[8]

Have students conduct a survey to see if people in their community agree with the results of the national sample. The question could be posed, Do you consider yourself an environmentalist? Have them ask follow-up questions to find out why these people consider themselves to be or not to be. Can individuals holding different values still be considered to have an environmental ethic? Students can also ask people in the community about their perceptions of other labels: conservationist, steward, nature lover, and preservationist.

Action Projects

Many projects can help students act on some of their beliefs, attitudes, and values. Action projects provide ways to examine values already held and can result in the clarification and formation of new values. Consider projects that improve environmental conditions and benefit the community in some way.

Activity 22. Taking Inventory

Before undertaking a project in the community, students should take an inventory of what is there, such as green spaces, buildings, bodies of water, and road networks. Deciding what to inventory in the local area and how to do it can reveal students' beliefs, attitudes, and values. Brainstorming a list of environmental issues and problems may raise questions about what actually exists there.

Have students develop a checklist and go out in teams to record this information. When they know more about the community, they can decide how to improve it. Consider improvements such as litter cleanups, bird and bat houses, erosion control, trail building, butterfly gardens, tree planting and pruning, stream check dams, and other projects.

What did you discover about the perceptions people hold in your community?

Activity 23. Master Planning

Planners have the responsibility for designing how change should take place in the community. When people decide they would like their communities to grow in orderly ways, planners are asked for suggestions on how this can be accomplished. When rules about growth and development are not in place, communities often evolve in ways that give nature little or low priority.

Have students find out what kinds of plans already exist in the community and how future growth and development are addressed. Investigate laws, ordinances, zoning regulations, building permits, and other ways to manage change. Are these planning mechanisms working well? If not, why not?

Obtain maps of the community (e.g., plat, vegetation, soil, topographic, political) and ask students to draw conclusions about the environmental ethics these maps reflect. Have them draft a community development policy statement(s) that reflects the ethics they believe should guide future development or land use issues. Using this policy as a guide, develop maps that show the best ways for the community to develop.

Be sure students can defend their plans, which should conform to their policy about preserving natural places. These master plans can be presented to the local planning commission or city council for their consideration and feedback.

How do master plans reflect values?

Creating Beauty

By using various forms of expression in the creative arts, students can develop their aesthetic and ethical values. Visual media can also communicate values about the land. Remember, beauty is in the eye of the beholder.

Activity 24. Navajo Chant

Part of a Navajo chant contains thoughts about beauty:

> May it be beautiful before me.
> May it be beautiful behind me.
> May it be beautiful below me.
> May it be beautiful above me.
> May it be beautiful all around me.

Beginning with classrooms, hallways, the cafeteria, and administrative offices, have students make a list of what is beautiful in their surroundings. There is a likelihood that different assessments of *beautiful* will arise. These diverse views will provide rich stimuli for discussions about aesthetic values. In the process of inventorying beauty, students may also identify what they consider *ugly*. These discoveries of beauty and ugliness can lead to future projects, adopt-a-highway cleanups, arrangement and design of the classroom, and other school site improvements.

Even though aesthetics is a separate area of philosophical study from ethics, the two are related. How?

Activity 25. Litter Sculptures

After collecting litter from the school grounds, park, or section of highway, students can create a sculpture from what has been discarded. These sculptures can be examples of what people do not value, but they also can be converted into creative forms that convey value messages. What messages do students want to communicate?

Before constructing the art piece, sort the discarded objects to analyze what each item implies about what people value or do not value. From this visual profile of community values and behaviors, ask students to describe the characteristics of the people who threw away the objects.

Do you agree with the concept there is no "away"?

Activity 26. Create an Image

For this activity, you may want to invest about three dollars for each kaleidoscope or you might consider helping students to make their own kaleidoscope using household materials. With either option, ask students to share their most beautiful designs and how they were created. Discuss why they value those designs.

What does "beauty is in the eye of the beholder" mean?

To purchase Create an Image kits, contact Gemini Kaleidoscopes, Zelienople, Pennsylvania 16063 (412-452-8700). These specially made kaleidoscopes have removable ends in which students can place tiny bits of natural or manufactured materials. Placing this collection of colors, textures, shapes, and forms in the tube and rotating yields beautiful patterns.

To make kaleidoscopes using common household materials, follow these steps:

- Measure and cut a $4\frac{1}{2}$" x 6" piece of previously used wrapping paper.

- Decorate a toilet paper tube by gluing the wrapping paper to the outside of the tube. Set aside.

- Measure and cut a 3" x $3\frac{1}{2}$" piece of card stock.

- Measure and cut a 3" x $3\frac{1}{2}$" piece of aluminum foil (or reflective Mylar).

- Place the aluminum foil (shiny or "mirror" side up) on top of the card stock. Tape the foil to the card stock by using transparent tape along the edges.

- Fold the foil-covered piece of card stock twice, lengthwise, to form a triangle or prism. Make sure the reflective or "mirrored" side of the prism faces inward. Secure with tape.

- Place 5 to 10 small objects (translucent objects work best) in a portion cup (used to hold ketchup or salad dressing at fast food restaurants). Place the lid on the portion cup tightly. (You may be able get a restaurant to sell or donate a small supply of these small, lidded portion cups.)

- Position the portion cup in one end of the toilet paper tube.

- Fold a paper towel in fourths and then wrap it completely around the prism. (You may need to trim the paper towel so it fits within the tube.)

- Fit the paper-towel-wrapped prism snugly in the center of the tube.

- Point the tube toward a light source and rotate. Light rays will cause the items placed in the portion cup to be reflected off the aluminum foil to form symmetrical patterns.[9]

Literature Springboards

Reading literature about the environment or stories involving nature can motivate students to explore their world with new eyes— and with new ideas. You might try reading a work together as a class or allowing students to select individual readings from a list. (Some books dealing with environmental ethics are mentioned in the bibliography.[10]) Allow students to reflect on what they've read by allowing them to participate in related outdoor group activities (or outdoor solitude). Provide opportunities for both individual and group experiences.

Activity 27. Letter from Planet Earth

Ask students to observe a place and imagine what message the Earth would have for today's youth if it could communicate with humans. Have them write a letter as though they were the Earth.[11]

Activity 28. Precious Gifts

Have students explore a place to find the most precious gift of nature and write a story (nonfiction or fiction) about that gift.[12]

Activity 29. Sacred Places

Ask students to go outside and find a place they would consider sacred (entitled to reverence and respect). Ask them to explain why they chose that place. Possible reasons for choosing a particular place might be the part it played in an important past event, pleasant personal experiences associated with it, a symbolic meaning, or aesthetic considerations.[13]

Activity 30. The Value of Trees

Living trees benefit ecosystems, provide shade, and are the source of many useful products. We usually focus more on the values of trees to humans than the values of trees to the plants and animals surrounding them.

Have students go outside and select a tree to observe. Ask them to imagine that plants and animals can whisper, and listen to what they say about the value of the tree. Have students write a story about what they say.[14]

Activity 31. Defending Nature

Natural areas are slowly shrinking in size and quality in many places in the world.

Encourage students to go outside and find something natural they value and would defend strongly if it were threatened. They should state why they think the place or object is valuable and how they would defend it.[15]

Activity 32. Counting Riches

Sometimes people confuse the idea of being rich or poor with whether or not they have money.

Ask students to go outside and tally the ways they are rich in nonmonetary ways. Have them note how difficult it is to place a dollar value on things such as a shady place to sit on a hot day, a colorful sunset, the pattern of a flower, or the services provided by elements in ecosystems.[16]

Activity 33. Organizational Muscle

Organizing to bring about needed changes has been an effective strategy for many years. One example is when Harriet Hemenway and Minna Hall formed the Audubon Society around the turn of the twentieth century. They wanted to prevent birds from being killed for feathers to decorate women's hats.

Have students make a survey of conservation and environmental organizations in the community. Find out if they have a specific mission to promote a particular cause or a more general mission to protect the environment.

If students identify an environmental issue they care about, they should consider forming a new organization or joining an existing one.[17]

Activity 34. Collecting Natural Pets

Collecting animals from nature and keeping them as pets may be considered a legal or ethical issue. In some cases, state or federal laws prohibit keeping wildlife pets without certain permits. Even when it is legal to capture and keep certain animals, some consider this practice unethical.

Urge students to investigate which local animals may be kept as pets. Visit a pet shop to find out about other wildlife that may be kept. After they discover what is legal, have students create a list of guiding principles to help them decide which animals it is ethical to keep.[18]

Activity 35. To Hunt or Not to Hunt

Hunting animals for food is a very old practice that has been necessary for human survival. Today hunting is controversial for several reasons. There are many variables to consider before deciding whether or not hunting is ethical. Why is this true? How can we find out what variables need consideration?

Help students construct a survey instrument that probes various hunting beliefs, attitudes, and values. There are lots of variables (e.g., gender, location, social context, age, ethnic and socioeconomic status) that influence how people respond to questions. Discuss how these variables affect the results of the survey. How can you use the demographic profile of the respondents to interpret the survey results? How would the species being hunted affect the responses?[19]

Activity 36. Purifying Pollution

Overpopulation has resulted in the pollution of air, soil, and water in many places in the world. The types of technologies used also determine the impact of human development on natural systems.

Have students trace the history of a local environmental problem. Find out pollution levels of the air, soil, and water. Determine the sources of contamination, how pollution is measured, and the estimated risks to human health.

How is *progress* determined? Does progress consider the effect of technologies on the health of the environment? If not, why not? Does the price of a product take into consideration the cost of reducing the pollution that results from its manufacture? How can an organization help clean up a polluted area?[20]

Games and Simulations

Play, creativity, and imagination are powerful tools for forming and shaping values and ethics. Games and simulations that use elements from nature can demonstrate ecological relationships or pose environmental ethic dilemmas.

Activity 37. Invent a Game

Invent a game that can be played inside or outside to teach others about the value of nature.

Consider ethical problems and issues such as picking plants, compacting the soil, threats to animal and plant species, eroding land, dying trees, animals bothering humans, disappearing natural areas, planning land use, and other issues. How can these issues be turned into a teaching game or simulation?

Explore computer simulations such as Sim-City or Sim-Earth. Are these accurate models for how the world works? How can certain games and simulations be improved to reflect reality more accurately?

Activity 38. Game-It, Name-It

Adapt an indoor game, like Monopoly, to be played outside. In the case of Monopoly, figure how the players can compensate (mitigate) for land being lost to development. After the game is adapted and played, ask questions:

- What could the penalties be, other than going to jail?
- Should society try to regulate the environmental behaviors of its members? If so, what is the best way to have society regulate the behaviors of others?
- Is education the best way to change beliefs, attitudes, and values, or are there other more effective ways?

Activity 39. Through the Eyes

Have students pretend that they are employed in different professions as they take a walk outside to view an area. Before going outside, they may wish to read about or talk to people who hold these different jobs. Instruct them to go outside and look at the land through the eyes and values of people in these various areas of employment.

Consider how the following people would value the land from their different perspectives: botanist, economist, gardener, historian, landscaper, mapmaker, musician, photographer, garbage collector, politician, visual artist, architect, author, engineer, ecologist, geologist, inventor, mathematician, naturalist, physician, poet, psychologist, teacher, farmer, and zoologist.

Is there a danger in stereotyping the kinds of values a person in a particular job might have? Explain.

Can any generalizations be made about how people in different professions value land?

What other kinds of jobs can be examined for their associated land values?[21]

Activity 40. Role Playing across the Environmental Ethics Continuum

How does the state of the environment look from different positions along the environmental ethics continuum?

Knowing their positions along this line helps students clarify their ethics. Have them role-play different perspectives by empathizing with others. This can help students respect various ways of viewing nature. For example, role-play an ecofeminist, a deep ecologist, a Wise Use movement member, a Leopold follower, and an ecoactivist. Role-play other perspectives as represented by different inhabitants of the world.

Notes

[1] Algernon D. Black, *The First Book of Ethics* (New York: Ethica Press, 1965), 35-38.

[2] To assist students in locating quotations, a good source is Barbara K. Rodes and Rice Odell, comp., *A Dictionary of Environmental Quotations* (New York: Simon & Schuster, 1992).

[3] For more bonding-with-nature activities, see Michael J. Cohen, *Reconnecting With Nature: Finding Wellness through Restoring Your Bond with the Earth* (Corvallis, OR: Ecopress, 1997).

[4] For more information about human impacts on nature, read William Rees and Mathis Wackernagel, *Our Ecological Footprint: Reducing Human Impact*

on the Earth (Gabriola Island, British Columbia: New Society Publishers, 1996).

[5] Good ideas for inventing observances and ceremonies can be found in Byrd Baylor, *I'm in Charge of Celebrations* (New York: Scribner's, 1986; reprint, Aladdin Paperbacks, 1995) and Cait Johnson and Maura D. Shaw, *Celebrating the Great Mother Earth: A Handbook of Earth-Honoring Activities for Parents and Children* (Rochester, VT: Destiny Books, 1995).

[6] For more ideas about questions to ask, see Kempton, Boster, and Hartley, *Environmental Values in American Culture*. For ideas about how to prepare questionnaires, see Hungerford et al., *Investigating and Evaluating Environmental Issues and Actions*.

[7] For further information, read Clifford Knapp, *Environmental Heroes and Heroines: An Instructional Unit in Earth Values and Ethics* (St. Paul: Pheasants Forever, 1993).

[8] Kempton, Boster, and Hartley, *Environmental Values in American Culture*, 216.

[9] These instructions were adapted, with permission, from an interdisciplinary guide developed by the *Voices* project. This activity guide connects science and math concepts with everyday events and objects (e.g., quilts, food preservation, traditional uses of plants and herbs). For ordering information, call AEL, 800-624-9120.

[10] In addition to the resources referenced in this section, many other books serve as springboards for exploring nature and the community. For more, see Clifford Knapp, *Just Beyond the Classroom: Community Adventures for Interdisciplinary Learning* (Charleston, WV: ERIC Clearinghouse on Rural Education and Small Schools, 1996), 87-88 or contact the Center for Children's Environmental Literature, 3603 Norton Place NW, Washington, DC 20016.

[11] Schim Schimmel, *Dear Children of the Earth: A Letter from Home* (Minocqua, WI: North Word Press, 1994).

[12] Ellen B. Jackson, *The Precious Gift: A Navajo Creation Myth* (New York: Simon & Schuster Books for Young Readers, 1996).

[13] Bruchac, *Between Earth & Sky*.

[14] Lynne Cherry, *The Great Kapok Tree: A Tale of the Amazon Rain Forest* (San Diego: Harcourt Brace Jovanovich, 1990). Books dealing with the value of ecosystem services include Yvonne Baskin, *The Work of Nature: How the Diversity of Life Sustains Us* (Washington, DC: Island Press, 1997) and Gretchen C. Daily, ed., *Nature's Services: Societal Dependence on Natural Ecosystems* (Washington, DC: Island Press, 1997). Contact Island Press, Box 7, Covelo, CA 95428, telephone 800-828-1302.

[15] Deborah Lee Rose, *The People Who Hugged the Trees: An Environmental Folk Tale* (Niwot, CO: Roberts Rinehart, 1990).

[16] Byrd Baylor, *The Table Where Rich People Sit.* (New York: Scribner's, 1994).

[17] Kathryn Lasky, *She's Wearing a Dead Bird on Her Head* (New York: Hyperion Paperbacks for Children, 1995).

[18] Anne Mazer, *The Salamander Room* (New York: Knopf, 1991).

[19] Paul Geraghty, *The Hunter* (New York: Crown, 1994).

[20]Lynne Cherry, *A River Ran Wild: An Environmental History* (San Diego: Harcourt Brace Jovanovich, 1992).

[21] For more suggestions, see Kathryn Sheehan and Mary Waidner, *Earth Child: Games, Stories, Activities, Experiments, & Ideas about Living Lightly on Planet Earth* (Tulsa: Council Oak Books, 1992).

CHAPTER 6

Selected Environmental Values and Ethics Resources

Very few curriculum materials focus specifically on environmental ethics. This chapter contains several sources for further information about environmental ethics curricula. Although these materials may not present a wide array of ethics across the human-centered/ Earth-centered continuum, they provide a starting point.

Environmental Ethics Curricular Resources

Approaching Environmental Issues in the Classroom by the National Consortium for Environmental Education and Training
   Kendall/Hunt Publishing Company
   4050 Westmark Drive, P.O. Box 1840
   Dubuque, IA 52004-1840
   Phone: 800-228-0810 (U.S.); 319-589-1000 (International)
   Fax: 800-772-9165 (U.S.); 319-589-1046 (International)

Biodiversity Basics: An Educator's Guide to Exploring the Web of Life
World Wildlife Fund
1250 24th Street, NW
Washington, DC 20037
Web site: http://www.wwf.org

"Bridging Science and the Humanities with Ethics"
c/o Carl F. Koch
Riverside Brookfield High School
160 Ridgewood Road
Riverside, IL 60546-2408
Phone: 708-442-7500
Fax: 708-447-5570
Web site: http://206.166.50.97/rbhs/home.htm

Ecodemia: Campus Environmental Stewardship at the Turn of the 21st Century, Lessons in Smart Management by Julian Keniry
National Wildlife Federation
8925 Leesburg Pike
Vienna, VA 22184
Phone: 800-477-5560 (ask for item #79866)
Web site: http://www.nwf.org/nwf/campus/ecodemia.html

Environmental Action
E2: Environment & Education
P.O. Box 20515
Boulder, CO 80308

"Environmental Ethics in Practice: Developing a Personal Ethic" by James E. Coufal and Charles M. Spuches
SUNY College of Environmental Science and Forestry
1 Forestry Drive
Syracuse, NY 13210
Phone: 315-470-6810
Web site: http://www.cep.unt.edu/news/practice.html

Environmental Heroes & Heroines: An Instructional Unit in Earth Values and Ethics by Clifford Knapp
  Pheasants Forever
  Leopold Education Project
  1783 Buerkle Circle
  St. Paul, MN 55110
  Phone: 651-773-2000
  Fax: 651-773-5500
  E-mail: lep@pheasantsforever.org
  Web site: http://www.lep.org/

Environmental Issues Forums (discussion guides on solid waste, wetlands, and water)
  Kendall/Hunt Publishing Company
  4050 Westmark Drive, P.O. Box 1840
  Dubuque, IA 52004-1840
  Phone: 800-228-0810 (U.S.); 319-589-1000 (International)
  Fax: 800-772-9165 (U.S.); 319-589-1046 (International)
  Web site: http://www.naaee.org/html/how_to_order.html

Environmental Respect
  Safari Club International
  4800 West Gates Pass Road
  Tucson, AZ 85745-9490
  Phone: 520-620-1220

From the Mountains to the Sea: A Journey in Environmental Citizenship
  Publications Section, Technology Development Branch
  Conservation and Protection
  Environment Canada
  Ottawa, Ontario K1A 0H3
  Phone: 613-998-4090
  Fax: 613-991-1634

Getting to Know the Wolf: A Teacher's Guide to the "Wolf-Pack" Materials
Yellowstone Association for Natural Science, History, and Education
P.O. Box 117
Yellowstone National Park, WY 82190
Phone: 307-344-7381

Home! A Bioregional Reader edited by Van Andruss, Christopher Plant, Judith Plant, and Eleanor Wright
New Society Publishers
P.O. Box 189
1680 Peterson Road
Gabriola Island, British Columbia V0R 1X0
Phone: 800-567-6772
Fax: 800-567-7311
E-mail: info@newsociety.com
Web site: http://www.newsociety.com/

Honoring Our Mother Earth
Green Timber Publications
P.O. Box 3884
Portland, ME 04104
Phone: 207-797-4180

Kids C.A.R.E.: A Cross-Curricular Environmental Program
(Grades 4-6)
Courthouse Plaza, NE
Dayton, OH 45463

Leopold Education Project
1783 Buerkle Circle
St. Paul, MN 55110
Phone: 651-773-2000
Fax: 651-773-5500
E-mail: lep@pheasantsforever.org
Web site: http://www.lep.org/

Opposing Viewpoints
   Greenhaven Press
   P.O. Box 289009
   San Diego, CA 82198-0009
   Phone: 800-231-5163

"People & Animals: A Humane Education Curriculum Guide"
   National Association for the Advancement of Humane Education
   67 Essex Turnpike
   East Haddam, CT 06423-1736
   Phone: 203-434-8666

"People-Animals and the Environment"
Contact your local animal welfare agency or:
   American Society for the Prevention of Cruelty to Animals
   424 East 92nd Street
   New York, NY 10128
   Web site: http://www.aspca.org/

Perspectives in Bioregional Education edited by Frank Traina and
Susan Darley-Hill (excellent resource section)
   North American Association for Environmental Education
   P.O. Box 400
   Troy, OH 45373
   Phone and Fax: 937-676-2514
   Web site: http://www.naaee.org/

Project LS: Land Stewardship and Lifestyle Decisions
   c/o Mary Norton
   Prairie Hills Farm
   New Hartford, IA 50660
   Phone: 319-983-2622

Project WILD
   707 Conservation Lane, Suite 305
   Gaithersburg, MD 20878
   Phone: 301-527-8900
   Fax: 301-527-8912
   E-mail: info@projectwild.org
   Web site: http://www.projectwild.org/

Rights to Responsibility: Multiple Approaches to Developing Character and Community by Alanda Greene
    Zephyr Press
    P.O. Box 66006
    Tucson, AZ 85728-6006
    Phone: 800-232-2187
    Fax: 520-323-9402
    E-mail: neways2learn@zephyrpress.com
    Web site: http://www.zephyrpress.com

River of Words Project (teacher's guide and information about the Environmental Poetry & Art Contest)
    International Rivers Network
    1847 Berkeley Way
    Berkeley, CA 94703
    Phone: 510-848-1155
    Fax: 510-848-1008
    E-mail: irnweb@irn.org
    Web site: http://www.irn.org/row/row.html

"Sustainable Forestry: Commitment to the Future, Educator's Packet"
    Wisconsin Department of Natural Resources, Bureau of Forestry
    P.O. Box 7921
    Madison, WI 53707-7921
    Phone: 608-267-7494

Teacher's Guide Units
    World Resources Institute
    1709 New York Avenue, NW
    Washington, DC 20006
    Phone: 202-638-6300
    Fax: 202-638-0036
    E-mail: valeriev@wri.org
    Web site: http://www.wri.org/cat-educ.html

This Land Is Sacred: A Teacher's Activity Guide to Environmental Ethics
North Carolina Wildlife Resources Commission
Division of Conservation Education
512 North Salisbury Street
Raleigh, NC 27604-1188
Phone: 919-733-7123

Trash Conflicts: A Science and Social Studies Curriculum on the Ethics of Disposal
Educators for Social Responsibility
23 Garden Street
Cambridge, MA 02138
Phone: 800-370-2515
Fax: 617-864-5164

The Wilderness & Land Ethic Box
Arthur Carhart National Wilderness Training Center
20325 Remount Road
Huson, MT 59846
Phone: 406-626-5208

Environmental Ethics Periodicals

Agriculture and Human Values
Kluwer Academic Publishers, Order Department
101 Philip Drive
Norwell, MA 02061
Phone: 781-871-6600
Fax: 781-871-6528
E-mail: kluwer@wkap.com
Web site: http://www.wkap.nl/journalhome.htm/0889-048X

The Amicus Journal
Natural Resources Defense Council
40 West 20th Street
New York, NY 10011
E-mail: amicus@nrdc.org

Audubon
National Audubon Society
700 Broadway
New York, NY 10003
Phone: 212-979-3000
Fax: 212-979-3188
E-mail: editor@audubon.org
Web site: http://magazine.audubon.org

Canadian Journal of Environmental Education
Arts and Science Division
Yukon College
Box 2799
Whitehorse, Yukon Y1A 5K4

Clearing: Environmental Education in the Pacific Northwest
Creative Educational Networks/Environmental Education Project
19600 South Molalla Avenue
Oregon City, OR 97045

Democracy & Nature
P.O. Box 637
Littleton, CO 80160-0637

Earth: The Science of Our Planet
Kalmback Publishing Company
21027 Crossroads Circle
Waukesha, WI 53186-4055

Earth Ethics
Center for Respect of Life and Environment
2100 L Street, NW
Washington, DC 20037
Phone: 202-778-6133
Fax: 202-778-6138
E-mail: crle@aol.com
Web site: http://www.center1.com/crle/ethics.html

The Ecologist
   The MIT Press
   55 Hayward Street
   Cambridge, MA 02142-1399
   Phone: 617-625-8569
   Fax: 617-625-6660
   E-mail: mitpress-orders@mit.edu
   Web site: http://mitpress.mit.edu/

Environmental Ethics
   Center for Environmental Philosophy
   P.O. Box 310980
   University of North Texas
   Denton, TX 76203-0980
   Phone: 940-565-2727
   Fax: 940-565-4439
   E-mail: ee@unt.edu
   Web site: http://www.cep.unt.edu/enethics.html

Environmental Values
   The White Horse Press
   1 STROND, Isle of Harris
   Scotland, HS5 3UD
   Phone and Fax: +44-1859-520-204
   E-mail: aj@erica.demon.co.uk
   Web site: http://www.erica.demon.co.uk/EV.html

E: The Environmental Magazine
   Earth Action Network
   Subscription Department
   P.O. Box 2047
   Marion, OH 43305-2047
   Phone: 815-734-1242
   E-mail: webmaster@emagazine.com
   Web site: http://www.emagazine.com/

Garbage: The Practical Journal for the Environment.
P.O. Box 51647
Boulder, CO 80321-1647

Green Teacher
P.O. Box 1431
Lewiston, NY 14092
Phone: 416-960-1244
Fax: 416-925-3474
E-mail: greentea@web.net
Web site: http://www.web.net/~greentea/index.html

Greenpeace USA
1436 U Street, NW
Washington, DC 20009
Phone: 202-462-1177
Fax: 202-462-4507
E-mail: greenpeace.usa@wdc.greenpeace.org
Web site: http://www.greenpeace.org/

Honor Digest
Honor Our Neighbors Origins and Rights
Route 1, Box 79-A
Bayfield, WI 54814

Human Education
National Association for the Advancement of Human Education
Division of the Humane Society of the United States
Norma Terris Humane Education Center
Box 362
East Haddam, CT 06423

Journal of Agricultural & Environmental Ethics
Kluwer Academic Publishers, Order Department
101 Philip Drive
Norwell, MA 02061
Phone: 781-871-6600
Fax: 781-871-6528
E-mail: kluwer@wkap.com

Journal of Environmental Education
  Heldref Publications
  1319 Eighteenth Street, NW
  Washington, DC 20036-1802
  Web site: http://www.heldref.org/

Legacy: The Magazine of the National Association of Interpretation
  Falcon Press Publishing
  P.O. Box 1718
  Helena, MT 59624

Mother Jones
  Subscription Department
  P.O. Box 469024
  Escondido, CA 92046
  Phone: 800-334-8152 (U.S.); 760-745-2809 (International)
  E-mail: subscribe@motherjones.com
  Web site: http://www.motherjones.com/

National Wildlife
  National Wildlife Federation
  8925 Leesburg Pike
  Vienna, VA 22184
  Phone: 800-477-5560
  Web site: http://www.nwf.org/

Nature Conservancy
  The Nature Conservancy
  1815 North Lynn Street
  Arlington, VA 22209
  Phone: 703-841-5300

News From Indian Country
  Route 2, Box 2900-A
  Hayward, WI 54843
  Phone: 715-634-5226

Orion Afield
   The Orion Society
   195 Main Street
   Great Barrington, MA 01230
   Phone: 888-909-6568
   Fax: 413-528-0676
   E-mail: orion@orionsociety.org
   Web site: http://orionsociety.org/afield.html

Orion Magazine
   The Orion Society
   195 Main Street
   Great Barrington, MA 01230
   Phone: 888-909-6568
   Fax: 413-528-0676
   E-mail: orion@orionsociety.org
   Web site: http://orionsociety.org/

Resources for the Future
   1616 P Street, NW
   Washington, DC 20036
   Phone: 202-328-5009

Taproot
   Coalition for Education in the Outdoors
   Park Center, P.O. Box 2000
   Cortland, NY 13045
   Phone: 607-753-4971
   Fax: 607-753-5982

Terra Nova: Nature & Culture
   The MIT Press
   55 Hayward Street
   Cambridge, MA 02142-1399
   Phone: 617-625-8569
   Fax: 617-625-6660
   E-mail: mitpress-orders@mit.edu
   Web site: http://mitpress.mit.edu

T.H.E. Journal: Technological Horizons in Education
150 El Camino Real, Suite 112
Tustin, CA 92780-3670

Whole Earth
P.O. Box 3000
Denville, NJ 07834-9879

Whole Terrain
Antioch New England Graduate School
40 Avon Street
Keene, NH 03431
Phone: 603-357-3122, extension 272
E-mail: whole_terrain@antiochne.edu
Web site: http://www.antiochne.edu/news_events/WT/issues.html

Worldviews: Environment, Culture, Religion
The White Horse Press
1 STROND, Isle of Harris
Scotland, HS5 3UD
Phone and Fax: +44-1859-520-204

World Watch
Worldwatch Institute
1776 Massachusetts Avenue, NW
Washington, DC 20036
Phone: 202-452-1999
Web site: http://www.worldwatch.org/mag/

A good source of information about environmental journals on the Internet can be found at http://www.cnie.org/Journals.htm. This site lists about 300 journals, including over 40 available in full text. The site is sponsored by the National Library for the Environment.

Afterword

As a teacher for more than 37 years, I have shared many rewarding outdoor learning moments with my students. Having now completed writing this book, I reflect on its contents. How can others make the best use of the ideas in this book? Have I helped to clarify these complex topics and to show how they are interrelated? Can this information be applied to create more rewarding learning moments for students in the future? As I thought about these questions, I remembered some of my experiences with nature and human nature over the years. These events have shaped my views about the importance of an environmental ethic.

More than 15 years ago, I developed a graduate course titled "Teaching Environmental Ethics." I was impelled to do this because I wanted teachers to think more about ethical questions and how they could help their students answer them. The teachers attending my classes asked for help in learning how to begin this adventure into largely unknown territory. They admitted having only limited knowledge about nature—from both the theoretical and experiential standpoints. Most had grown up in cities where nature had been squeezed into postage-stamp-sized parks. Their direct contacts with nature had been mediated by various forms of modern technology. They had not explored much philosophy either, especially the applied field of environmental ethics. They knew quite a bit about teaching for skill and concept development, but teaching for values and ethics development was unfamiliar to most. They knew little of the wide range of ethical views regarding nature or had little experience in handling controversial issues in their classrooms. Getting in touch with the community's beliefs, attitudes, and values related to the environment was difficult. In their teacher education preparation, my students were not encouraged to venture far beyond the safe and accepted topics of the noncontroversial, subject-matter-based curriculum. Through this graduate course over the years, I tried to help my students expand their understandings of these diverse and somewhat slippery concepts and practices.

I had long been an advocate of values clarification and used it often in my teaching. I knew I had learned many of my values by thinking, sharing, and doing something about them with others.

However, I still felt some confusion and discomfort over how I should teach about and for values. I wanted my students to share my love for the outdoors and my desire to protect the natural world. On the other hand, my conscience warned that I had no right to inculcate the students with all of my values. Where should I draw the line? What was I to do? How could I handle this obvious internal conflict?

After pondering these questions, I decided I had trapped myself in a paralyzing dualism. For years, I thought I had to hide my feelings in the classroom to teach about controversial issues. I thought I had to wear two hats—one in the classroom belonging to an objective educator and another at home belonging to a passionate environmentalist. I knew my students were too intelligent to be fooled by ingenuine role playing. To solve this dilemma, I worked hard at learning how to create humane and safe learning communities. In this type of supportive group, we could freely express our values and also celebrate our differences. I finally came to realize I could continue to share my enthusiasm, love, and respect for the land and still honor the diversity of values and ethics in my students. I no longer had to hide my feelings and beliefs. I no longer had to teach from only one side of my brain and from under only one hat. That is why I included a brief section on building humane learning communities in this book. I knew that doing this was one of the keys to feeling successful in helping others develop their environmental ethics.

I remember one student in particular who helped me do a lot of thinking and growing. The class structure supported Darrin to express freely his decidedly human-centered worldviews. I knew if I tried to suppress his thoughts and feelings, he would find the class unrewarding and tension filled. In an oppressive educational climate, no one learns very much. Largely because Darrin was there, we had many stimulating discussions about environmental ethics. All of the students shared my excitement when we presented our diverse views about nature/human nature interactions. We learned a lot about how to maintain a sense of community despite a diversity of opinions. We also learned about the power of engaging in discussions about controversial issues.

It is probably evident now that the process of developing an environmental ethic cannot be neatly wrapped into a tight cognitive package and dispensed sequentially to students. I hope this book will encourage you to begin integrating environmental ethics into the curriculum.

I have been accused of being a hopeless optimist, but I firmly believe that if we demonstrate humanity's destructive and constructive potential, students will shift their environmental ethics in life-saving directions. I may be naive and idealistic, but I have great faith in the creative abilities of humans to make the right survival choices under the right conditions. Being an optimist does not mean denying that humans have made some errors. We need to push toward a vision of how we can maintain harmony with the rest of nature. It also means being gentle on ourselves when we fall short of our ideals.

I want to continue to immerse my students in positive, out-of-classroom experiences in urban, suburban, and rural settings. I want to help them reflect on these experiences in supportive learning communities so they can apply these ideas to their lives. I want to facilitate the sharing of insights spanning the range of human relationships to nature over the centuries. I want to open the doors so my students can explore new territory, and in the process, they can feel the excitement and enrichment new knowledge can bring to the human experience.

There are many opportunities to apply rational and critical thinking in developing an ethic. However, I always need to remember that forming an environmental ethic extends beyond the cognitive realm to include the attitudes, values, feelings, and actions involved in gathering and producing knowledge. The following words point to the power of teaching and the interconnected components of ethics formation:

> *In the end . . .*
> We will conserve only what we love
> We will love only what we understand
> *We will understand only what we are taught*
> —Baba Dioum, Senegal proverb

> *Watch your thoughts; they become words.*
> Watch your words; they become actions.
> Watch your actions; they become habits.
> Watch your habits; they become character.
> *Watch your character; it becomes your destiny.*
> —Frank Outlaw

Our destiny on this planet will be determined by how our love, understandings, thoughts, words, actions, habits, and character shape our relationships with the Earth and how we are taught. The challenge is ours. I hope you accept your part.

Bibliography

Abbey, Edward. *Desert Solitaire: A Season in the Wilderness.* New York: McGraw-Hill, 1968. Reprint, New York: Simon & Schuster, 1990.

———. *A Voice Crying in the Wilderness: Notes from a Secret Journal.* New York: St. Martin's Press, 1990.

Abram, David. *The Spell of the Sensuous: Perception and Language in a More-Than-Human World.* New York: Pantheon Books, 1996.

American Geological Institute. *Essence I.* Rev. ed. New York: Addison-Wesley Publishing Company, 1971.

Andruss, Van, Christopher Plant, Judith Plant, and Eleanor Wright, eds. *Home! A Bioregional Reader.* Philadelphia: New Society Publishers, 1990.

Ayers, William, Jean Ann Hunt, and Therese Quinn, eds. *Teaching for Social Justice: A* Democracy and Education *Reader.* New York: New Press and Teachers College Press, 1998.

Baltic, Tony. "Technology and the Evolution of Land Ethics." In *Nature and the Human Spirit: Toward an Expanded Land Management Ethic,* edited by B. L. Driver, Daniel Dustin, Tony Baltic, Gary Elsner, and George Peterson. State College, PA: Venture Publishing, 1996.

Bardwell, Lisa A., Martha C. Monroe, and Margaret T. Tudor. *Environmental Problem Solving: Theory, Practice and Possibilities in Environmental Education.* Troy, OH: North American Association for Environmental Education, 1994.

Baskin, Yvonne. *The Work of Nature: How the Diversity of Life Sustains Us.* Washington, DC: Island Press, 1997.

Baylor, Byrd. *I'm in Charge of Celebrations.* New York: Scribner's, 1986. Reprint, Aladdin Paperbacks, 1995.

———. *The Table Where Rich People Sit.* New York: Scribner's, 1994.

Beatley, Timothy. *Ethical Land Use: Principles of Policy and Planning.* Baltimore: Johns Hopkins University Press, 1994.

Bellah, Robert N., Richard Madsen, William M. Sullivan, Ann Swidler, and Stephen M. Tipton. *Habits of the Heart: Individualism and Commitment in American Life.* Berkeley: University of California Press, 1985. Updated with a new introduction, Berkeley: University of California Press, 1996.

Berg, Peter. "More Than Just Saving What's Left." In *Home! A Bioregional Reader,* edited by Van Andruss, Christopher Plant, Judith Plant, and Eleanor Wright. Philadelphia: New Society Publishers, 1990.

Berry, Wendell. *Home Economics: Fourteen Essays.* San Francisco: North Point Press, 1987.

Black, Algernon D. *The First Book of Ethics.* New York: Franklin Watts, 1965.

Bookchin, Murray. *The Modern Crisis.* Philadelphia: New Society Publishers, 1986.

———. "What Is Social Ecology?" In *Environmental Philosophy: From Animal Rights to Radical Ecology,* edited by Michael E. Zimmerman. Englewood Cliffs, NJ: Prentice Hall, 1993.

Bowers, C. A. *Educating for an Ecologically Sustainable Culture: Rethinking Moral Education, Creativity, Intelligence, and Other Modern Orthodoxies.* Albany: State University of New York Press, 1995.

Bramwell, Anna. *Ecology in the 20th Century: A History.* New Haven, CT: Yale University Press, 1989.

Bruchac, Joseph. *Between Earth & Sky: Legends of Native American Sacred Places.* San Diego: Harcourt Brace & Co., 1996.

Caduto, Michael J. *A Guide on Environmental Values Education.* Paris, France: UNESCO, 1985.

Carson, Rachel. *The Sense of Wonder.* New York: Harper & Row, 1956.

Charles, Cheryl. "Creating Community: What Is It and How Do We Do It? The Emerging Story of the Center for the Study of Community." Paper presented at the Eighth International Conference of the International Association for the Study of Cooperation in Education, Lewis and Clark College, Portland, OR, 10 July 1994.

Cheney, Jim. "Eco-Feminism and Deep Ecology." *Environmental Ethics* 9 (summer 1987): 115-45.

Cherry, Lynne. *The Great Kapok Tree: A Tale of the Amazon Rain Forest.* San Diego: Harcourt Brace Jovanovich, 1990.

———. *A River Ran Wild: An Environmental History.* San Diego: Harcourt Brace Jovanovich, 1992.

Cohen, Michael J. *Reconnecting with Nature: Finding Wellness through Restoring Your Bond with the Earth.* Corvallis, OR: Ecopress, 1997.

Commoner, Barry. *The Closing Circle: Confronting the Environmental Crisis.* London: Cape, 1972.

Corcoran, Peter B., and Eric Sievers. "Reconceptualizing Environmental Education: Five Possibilities." *Journal of Environmental Education* 25 (summer 1994): 4-8.

Cornell, Joseph. *Listening to Nature: How to Deepen Your Awareness of Nature.* Nevada City, CA: Dawn Publications, 1987.

Cwiklik, Robert, ed. "Class Wars: Are Computers the Saviors of Education? It Depends on Whom You Ask." *The Wall Street Journal,* 17 November 1997.

Daily, Gretchen C., ed. *Nature's Services: Societal Dependence on Natural Ecosystems.* Washington, DC: Island Press, 1997.

Deloria, Vine, Jr. *God Is Red: A Native View of Religion*. 2d ed. Golden, CO: North American Press, 1992.

DesJardins, Joseph R. *Environmental Ethics: An Introduction to Environmental Philosophy*. Belmont, CA: Wadsworth, 1993.

Dewey, John. *Experience and Education*. 1938. Reprint, West Lafayette, IN: Kappa Delta Pi, 1998.

———. *The School and Society*. 1899. Reprint (includes *The Child and the Curriculum*), Chicago: University of Chicago Press, 1990.

Diamond, Irene, and Gloria Feman Orenstein, eds. *Reweaving the World: The Emergence of Ecofeminism*. San Francisco: Sierra Club Books, 1990.

Driver, B. L., Daniel Dustin, Tony Baltic, Gary Elsner, and George Peterson, eds. *Nature and the Human Spirit: Toward an Expanded Land Management Ethic*. State College, PA: Venture Publishing, 1996.

Durning, Alan Thein. *This Place on Earth: Home and the Practice of Permanence*. Seattle: Sasquatch Books, 1996.

Engleson, David C., and Dennis H. Yockers. *Environmental Education: A Guide to Curriculum Planning*. 2d ed. Bulletin 94371. Madison: Wisconsin State Department of Public Instruction, 1994. ERIC Document Reproduction Service No. ED 380 306.

Evernden, Neil. *The Social Creation of Nature*. Baltimore: Johns Hopkins University Press, 1992.

Fine, Melinda. *Habits of the Mind: Struggling over Values in America's Classrooms*. San Francisco: Jossey-Bass, 1995.

Foreman, David. *Confessions of an Eco-Warrior*. New York: Harmony Books, 1991.

———. "The New Conservation Movement." In *Deep Ecology for the Twenty-First Century*, edited by George Sessions. Boston: Shambhala, 1995.

Frankena, William K. "Ethics and the Environment." In *Ethics and Problems of the 21st Century*, edited by K. E. Goodpaster and K. M. Sayre. Notre Dame, IN: University of Notre Dame Press, 1979.

Free, Ann Cottrell, ed. *Animals, Nature, and Albert Schweitzer*. New York: A. Schweitzer Fellowship, 1982.

Gardner, John W. *Building Community*. Washington, DC: Leadership Studies Program of Independent Sector, 1991.

Geraghty, Paul. *The Hunter*. New York: Crown, 1994.

Glenn, Kelly V., ed. *The Free Market Environmental Bibliography*. 4th ed. Washington, DC: Competitive Enterprise Institute, 1996.

Gore, Al. *Earth in the Balance: Ecology and the Human Spirit*. Boston: Houghton Mifflin, 1992. Reprint, New York: Plume, 1993.

Gray, Elizabeth Dodson. "Come Inside the Circle of Creation: An Ethic of Attunement." In *Ethics and Environmental Policy: Theory Meets*

Practice, edited by Frederick Ferre and Peter Hartel. Athens: University of Georgia Press, 1994.

Griffin, Susan. Quoted in *Confessions of an Eco-Warrior*, by David Foreman. New York: Harmony Books, 1991.

Guebert, Alan. "AG Biotech: Just Because We Can?" *CountryView*, 31 March 1998, 8.

Haeckel, Ernst. *General Morphology of Organisms*. N.p., 1866.

Hammond, William F. *Acting on Action as an Integral Component of Schooling*. Ft. Myers, FL: Natural Context, 1993.

———. "Action Within Schools." In *Environmental Problem Solving*, edited by Lisa V. Bardwell, Martha C. Monroe, and Margaret T. Tudor. Troy, OH: North American Association for Environmental Education, 1994.

Hargrove, Eugene C., ed. *The Animal Rights, Environmental Ethics Debate: The Environmental Perspective*. Albany: State University of New York Press, 1992.

Harjo, Joy. *Secrets from the Center of the World*. Tucson: University of Arizona Press, Sun Tracks, 1989.

Harvey, Karen D., Lisa D. Harjo, and Jane K. Jackson. *Teaching about Native Americans*. Washington, DC: National Council for the Social Studies, 1990.

Harvey, Karen D., Lisa D. Harjo, and Lynda Welborn. *How to Teach about American Indians: A Guide for the School Library Media Specialist*. Westport, CT: Greenwood Press, 1995.

Hiss, Tony. *The Experience of Place*. New York: Knopf, 1990. Reprint, New York: Vintage Books, 1991.

Hungerford, Harold, and Trudi L. Volk. "The Challenges of K-12 Environmental Education." In *Monographs in Environmental Education and Environmental Studies, Volume I*, edited by Arthur B. Sacks. Columbus, OH: ERIC Clearinghouse for Science, Mathematics, and Environmental Education, 1984. ERIC Document Reproduction Service No. ED 251 293.

Hungerford, Harold, R. Ben Peyton, John Ramsey, and Trudi L. Volk. *Investigating and Evaluating Environmental Issues and Actions: Skill Development Modules*. Champaign, IL: Stipes Publishing L.L.C., 1992. ERIC Document Reproduction Service No. ED 368 557.

Hungerford, Harold R., William J. Bluhm, Trudi L. Volk, and John Ramsey. *Essential Readings in Environmental Education*. Champaign, IL: Stipes Publishing L.L.C., 1998.

Independent Commission on Environmental Education. *Are We Building Environmental Literacy? A Report by the Independent Commission on Environmental Education*. Washington, DC: George C. Marshall Institute, 1997.

Jackson, Ellen B. *The Precious Gift: A Navajo Creation Myth*. New York: Simon & Schuster Books for Young Readers, 1996.

Jenkins, Edgar W. "Gender and Science & Technology Education." *Connect UNESCO International Science, Technology & Environmental Education Newsletter* 22 (1997): 1, 3.

Johnson, Cait, and Maura D. Shaw. *Celebrating the Great Mother: A Handbook of Earth-Honoring Activities for Parents and Children.* Rochester, VT: Destiny Books, 1995.

Kaplan, Rachel, and Stephen Kaplan. *The Experience of Nature: A Psychological Perspective.* New York: Cambridge University Press, 1989.

Kellert, Stephen R. *Kinship to Mastery: Biophilia in Human Evolution and Development.* Washington, DC: Island Press, 1997.

———. "Social and Psychological Dimensions of an Environmental Ethic." In *Proceedings of the International Conference on Outdoor Ethics.* Arlington, VA: Izaak Walton League of America, 1987.

Kempton, Willett, James S. Boster, and Jennifer A. Hartley. *Environmental Values in American Culture.* Cambridge, MA: MIT Press, 1996.

King, Ynestra. "Healing the Wounds: Feminism, Ecology, and the Nature/Culture Dualism." In *Reweaving the World: The Emergence of Ecofeminism*, edited by Irene Diamond and Gloria Feman Orenstein. San Francisco: Sierra Club Books, 1990.

Kirschenbaum, Howard. *100 Ways to Enhance Values and Morality in Schools and Youth Settings.* Boston: Allyn and Bacon, 1995.

Kline, Benjamin. *First Along the River: A Brief History of the United States Environmental Movement.* San Francisco: Acada Books, 1997.

Knapp, Clifford. *Environmental Heroes and Heroines: An Instructional Unit in Earth Values and Ethics.* St. Paul: Pheasants Forever, 1993.

———. "Images of Nature." *Nature Study* 45 (June 1992): 44-47.

———. *Just Beyond the Classroom: Community Adventures for Interdisciplinary Learning.* Charleston, WV: ERIC Clearinghouse on Rural Education and Small Schools, 1996. ERIC Document Reproduction Service No. ED 388 485.

Kohlberg, Lawrence. "Continuities in Childhood and Adult Moral Development Revisited." In *Life-Span Developmental Psychology: Personality and Socialization*, edited by Paul B. Baltes and K. Warner Schaie. New York: Academic Press, 1973.

———. "Stages of Moral Development as a Basis for Moral Education." In *Moral Education: Interdisciplinary Approaches*, edited by C. M. Beck, B. S. Critenden, and E. V. Sullivan. Toronto: University of Toronto Press, 1971.

Lasky, Kathryn. *She's Wearing a Dead Bird on Her Head.* New York: Hyperion Books for Children, 1995.

Leopold, Aldo. *The River of the Mother of God and Other Essays by Aldo Leopold.* Edited by Susan L. Flader and J. Baird Callicott. Madison: University of Wisconsin Press, 1991.

———. *A Sand County Almanac and Sketches Here and There.* 1949. Reprint, New York: Oxford University Press, 1987.

———. "Teaching Wildlife Conservation in Public Schools." *Transactions of the Wisconsin Academy of Sciences, Arts, and Letters* 30 (1937): 77-86.

Levin, Jack, and James L. Spates. *Starting Sociology.* 3d ed. New York: Harper & Row, 1985.

Lickona, Thomas. *Educating for Character: How Our Schools Can Teach Respect and Responsibility.* New York: Bantam, 1991.

List, Peter C., ed. *Radical Environmentalism: Philosophy and Tactics.* Belmont, CA: Wadsworth, 1993.

Machlis, Gary. "Outdoor Ethics in America." In *Proceedings of the International Conference on Outdoor Ethics.* Arlington, VA: Izaak Walton League of America, 1987.

Mander, Jerry. *In the Absence of the Sacred: The Failure of Technology and the Survival of the Indian Nations.* San Francisco: Sierra Club Books, 1991.

Maslow, Abraham H. *Toward a Psychology of Being.* 3d ed. New York: J. Wiley & Sons, 1998.

Matthews, Bruce E., and Cheryl K. Riley. *Teaching and Evaluating Outdoor Ethics Education Programs.* Vienna, VA: National Wildlife Federation, 1995. ERIC Document Reproduction Service No. ED 401 097.

Mazer, Anne. *The Salamander Room.* New York: Knopf, 1991.

McClaren, Milton. "After Earth Day 1990 . . . What?" In *The Best of Clearing: Environmental Education in the Pacific Northwest, Vol. IV,* edited by Larry Beutler. Oregon City, OR: The Environmental Project, 1993.

———. Letter to author.

McKibben, Bill. *The End of Nature.* New York: Random House, 1989.

Merchant, Carolyn. "The Death of Nature." In *From Animal Rights to Radical Ecology,* edited by Michael E. Zimmerman. Englewood Cliffs, NJ: Prentice Hall, 1993.

———. "Ecofeminism and Feminist Theory." In *Reweaving the World: The Emergence of Ecofeminism,* edited by Irene Diamond and Gloria Feman Orenstein. San Francisco: Sierra Club Books, 1990.

Miller, G. Tyler, Jr. *Living in the Environment: An Introduction to Environmental Science.* 5th ed. Belmont, CA: Wadsworth, 1988.

Mills, Stephanie. Foreword to *Home! A Bioregional Reader,* edited by Van Andruss, Christopher Plant, Judith Plant, and Eleanor Wright. Philadelphia: New Society Publishers, 1990.

———. "Thoughts from the Round River Rendezvous." *Earth First!* 2 February 1986, 25.

Momaday, N. Scott. "A First American Views His Land." *National Geographic* 150 (July 1976): 13-19.

Muir, John. *The Story of My Boyhood and Youth.* 1913. Reprint, San Francisco: Sierra Club Books, 1988.

———. *A Thousand-Mile Walk to the Gulf.* 1916. Reprint, New York: Penguin Books, 1992.

Mumford, Lewis. *The Myth of the Machine.* New York: Harcourt Brace & World, 1967.

———. *The Pentagon of Power.* New York: Harcourt Brace Jovanovich, 1970.

———. *The Transformations of Man.* New York: Harper, 1956.

Nabhan, Gary Paul, and Stephen Trimble. *The Geography of Childhood: Why Children Need Wild Places.* Boston: Beacon Press, 1994.

Naess, Arne. "The Deep Ecological Movement: Some Philosophical Aspects." In *Environmental Philosophy: From Animal Rights to Radical Ecology,* edited by Michael E. Zimmerman. Englewood Cliffs, NJ: Prentice Hall, 1993. Reprint, Upper Saddle River, NJ: Prentice Hall, 1998.

Nash, Roderick F. "Aldo Leopold's Intellectual Heritage." In *Companion to A Sand County Almanac: Interpretive & Critical Essays,* edited by J. Baird Callicott. Madison: University of Wisconsin Press, 1987.

———. *The Rights of Nature: A History of Environmental Ethics.* Madison: University of Wisconsin Press, 1989.

National Environmental Education Advisory Council. *Report Assessing Environmental Education in the United States and the Implementation of the National Environmental Education Act of 1990.* Washington, DC: U.S. Environmental Protection Agency, Environmental Education Division, 1996.

Orr, David W. *Ecological Literacy: Education and the Transition to a Postmodern World.* Albany: State University of New York Press, 1992.

Peck, M. Scott. *The Different Drum: Community-Making and Peace.* New York: Simon and Schuster, 1987.

Piaget, Jean. *The Child's Conception of the World.* 1929. Reprint, Paterson, NJ: Littlefield, Adams, 1963.

———. *The Origins of Intelligence in Children.* New York: International Universities Press, 1952.

———. *Six Psychological Studies.* New York: Random House, 1967.

Pinchot, Gifford. *Breaking New Ground.* 1947. Reprint, Washington, DC: Island Press, 1998.

———. *The Fight for Conservation.* 1910. Reprint, Seattle: University of Washington Press, 1967.

———. Quoted in *Dreamers and Defenders: American Conservationists,* by Douglas H. Strong. Lincoln: University of Nebraska Press, 1995.

Postman, Neil. *The End of Education: Redefining the Value of School.* New York: Knopf, 1995.

———. *Technopoly: The Surrender of Culture to Technology.* New York: Knopf, 1992.

Quinn, Daniel. *Ishmael: A Novel.* New York: Bantam/Turner Books, 1992.

Raths, Louis E., Merrill Harmin, and Sidney B. Simon. *Values and Teaching: Working with Values in the Classroom.* 2d ed. Columbus, OH: C. E. Merrill Publishing Company, 1978.

Regan, Tom. "Animal Rights, Human Wrongs." In *Environmental Philosophy: From Animal Rights to Radical Ecology,* edited by Michael E. Zimmerman. Englewood Cliffs, NJ: Prentice Hall, 1993.

———. *The Case for Animal Rights.* Berkeley: University of California Press, 1983.

Rees, William, and Mathis Wackernagel. *Our Ecological Footprint: Reducing Human Impact on the Earth.* Gabriola Island, British Columbia: New Society Publishers, 1996.

Reimer, Joseph, Diana Pritchard Paolitto, and Richard H. Hersh. *Promoting Moral Growth: From Piaget to Kohlberg.* 2d ed. New York: Longman, 1983.

Riley, Richard. "Closing the Distance." *Teaching pre-K-8* 28 (January 1998): 6.

Robottom, Ian. "Beyond the Model/Module Mentality." In *Environmental Problem Solving,* edited by Lisa V. Bardwell, Martha C. Monroe, and Margaret T. Tudor. Troy, OH: North American Association for Environmental Education, 1994.

Rodes, Barbara K., and Rice Odell, comp. *A Dictionary of Environmental Quotations.* New York: Simon & Schuster, 1992.

Rogers, Carl R. "Toward a Modern Approach to Values: The Valuing Process in the Mature Person." In *Readings in Values Clarification,* compiled by Sidney B. Simon and Howard Kirschenbaum. Minneapolis: Winston Press, 1973.

Roggenbuck, Joseph, and B. L. Driver. "Public Land Management Agencies, Environmental Education, and an Expanded Land Management Ethic." In *Nature and the Human Spirit,* edited by B. L. Driver, Daniel Dustin, Tony Baltic, Gary Elsner, and George Peterson. State College, Pa.: Venture Publishing, 1996.

Rohwedder, W. J., and Andy Alm. *Using Computers in Environmental Education: Interactive Multimedia and On-Line Learning.* Ann Arbor: Michigan University School of Natural Resources and Environment, National Consortium for Environmental Education and Training, 1994.

Rolston, Holmes, III. "Valuing Wildlands." *Environmental Ethics* 7 (Spring 1985): 23-48.

Rose, Deborah Lee. *The People Who Hugged the Trees: An Environmental Folk Tale.* Niwot, CO: Roberts Rinehart, 1990.

Roszak, Theodore. *The Voice of the Earth*. New York: Simon & Schuster, 1992.

Ryan, Kevin. "The New Moral Education." *Phi Delta Kappan* 68 (November 1986): 228-33.

Schimmel, Schim, *Dear Children of the Earth: A Letter from Home*. Minocqua, WI: North Word Press, 1994.

Schweitzer, Albert. "Biocentric Ethics." In *Environmental Ethics: Readings in Theory and Application*, edited by Louis P. Pojman. Boston: Jones and Bartlett, 1994.

———. *Indian Thought and Its Development*. Translated by Mrs. Charles E. B. Russell. New York: H. Holt and Company, 1936.

———. *Out of My Life and Thought: An Autobiography*. 1933. Reprint, Baltimore: Johns Hopkins University Press, 1998.

Seed, John, Joanna Macy, Pat Fleming, and Arne Naess. *Thinking Like a Mountain: Towards a Council of All Beings*. Philadelphia: New Society Publishers, 1988.

Sergiovanni, Thomas J. *Building Community in Schools*. San Francisco: Jossey-Bass, 1994.

Sessions, George, ed. *Deep Ecology for the Twenty-First Century*. Boston: Shambhala, 1995.

Sheehan, Kathryn, and Mary Waidner. *Earth Child: Games, Stories, Activities, Experiments, & Ideas about Living Lightly on Planet Earth*. Tulsa: Council Oaks Books, 1992.

Shrader-Frechette, K. S. *Environmental Ethics*. Pacific Grove, CA: The Boxwood Press, 1981.

Silko, Leslie Marmon. *Almanac of the Dead: A Novel*. New York: Simon & Schuster, 1991.

———. *Ceremony*. New York: Viking Press, 1977. Reprint, New York: Penguin Books, 1986.

———. *Storyteller*. New York: Seaver Books, 1981.

Singer, Peter. *Animal Liberation: A New Ethics for Our Treatment of Animals*. New York: New York Review, 1975.

Smith, Gregory A. *Education and the Environment: Learning to Live with Limits*. Albany: State University of New York Press, 1992.

Sobel, David. *Children's Special Places: Exploring the Role of Forts, Dens, and Bush Houses in Middle Childhood*. Tucson: Zephyr Press, 1993. ERIC Document Reproduction Service No. ED 369 558.

Spranger, Michael S. "Global Environmental Values and Ethics: A Challenge for Educators." Paper presented at National Science Foundation Middle School Teacher Training Workshop, Biloxi, MS, 18 June 1993.

Staniforth, Susan. *The Technology Trap, Module 1 Transportation: Who's in the Driver's Seat?* Victoria, British Columbia: Sierra Club of

British Columbia, Salvadoran Centre for Appropriate Technology, 1997.

Stapp, William B., and Arjen E. J. Wals. "An Action Research Approach to Environmental Problem Solving." In *Environmental Problem Solving*, edited by Lisa V. Bardwell, Martha C. Monroe, and Margaret T. Tudor. Troy, OH: North American Association for Environmental Education, 1994.

Stoll, Clifford. *Silicon Snake Oil: Second Thoughts on the Information Highway.* New York: Doubleday, 1995.

Strong, David. *Crazy Mountains: Learning from Wilderness to Weigh Technology.* Albany: State University of New York Press, 1995.

Strong, Douglas H. *Dreamers and Defenders: American Conservationists.* Lincoln: University of Nebraska Press, 1988.

Suzuki, David, and Peter Knudtson. *Wisdom of the Elders: Honoring Sacred Native Visions of Nature.* New York: Bantam Books, 1992.

Swan, James A. *Nature as Teacher and Healer: How to Reawaken Your Connection with Nature.* New York: Villard Books, 1992.

Taylor, Paul W. *Respect for Nature: A Theory of Environmental Ethics.* Princeton, NJ: Princeton University Press, 1986.

Thoreau, Henry David. *The Heart of Thoreau's Journals.* Edited by Odell Shepard. 1927. Reprint, New York: Dover Publications, 1961.

———. *The Portable Thoreau.* Rev. ed. Edited by Carl Bode. New York: Penguin Books, 1977.

Toffler, Alvin. *Future Shock.* New York: Random House, 1970.

Tönnies, Ferdinand. *Gemeinschaft und Gesellschaft.* Leipzig: Fues, 1887. Translated and edited by C. P. Loomis under the title of *Community and Society.* East Lansing: Michigan State University, 1957. Reprint, New Brunswick, NJ: Transaction Books, 1988.

United Nations Environment Program. *World Charter for Nature.* Paris: United Nations Environment Program, 1982.

VanDeVeer, Donald, and Christine Pierce, eds. *People, Penguins, and Plastic Trees: Basic Issues in Environmental Ethics.* Belmont, CA: Wadsworth, 1986.

Varner, Gary. "The Role of Environmental Ethics in Environmental Education." In *Environmental Ethics: Strategies for Implementation—Nonformal Workshop,* edited by C. H. Yaple. Orlando, FL: National Association for Environmental Education, 1988.

Wachtel, Paul L. *The Poverty of Affluence: A Psychological Portrait of the American Way of Life.* New York: Free Press, 1983.

Wade, Rahima C., ed. *Community Service-Learning: A Guide to Including Service in the Public School Curriculum.* Albany: State University of New York Press, 1997.

Warren, Karen J. "Feminism and Ecology: Making Connections." *Environmental Ethics* 9 (spring 1987): 3-20.

———. "The Power and the Promise of Ecological Feminism." *Environmental Ethics* 12 (summer 1990): 125-46.

———. "Warren's Proposed Model for Thinking and Writing about Environmental Issues, Ethics, and Actions." Paper presented at Macalester College, St. Paul, MN, 20 January 1993.

Warren, Roland L. "The Good Community—What Would It Be? In *Perspectives on the American Community,* 2d ed., edited by Roland L. Warren. Chicago: Rand McNally, 1973.

Watson, Paul, and Peter Dykstra. "Greenpeace." *Environment* 28 (July-August 1986): 45.

Watson, Paul, and Warren Rogers. *Sea Shepherd: My Fight for Whales and Seals.* Edited by Joseph Newman. New York: Norton, 1982.

Weilbacher, Mike. "The Single Most Important Thing to Know about the Earth (and It's Probably Not What You Think)." *Clearing* 85 (September/October 1994): 3-4.

Westheimer, Joel, and Joseph Kahne. "Building School Communities: An Experience-Based Model." *Phi Delta Kappan* 75 (December 1993): 324-28.

White, Lynn, Jr. "The Historical Roots of Our Ecologic Crisis." *Science* 155 (10 March 1967): 1203-07.

Wilke, Richard J., ed. *Environmental Education Teacher Resource Handbook: A Practical Guide for K-12 Environmental Education.* Millwood, NY: Kraus International Publications, 1993.

Wilson, Edward O. *Naturalist.* Washington, DC: Island Press/Shearwater Books, 1994.

Yambert, Paul A., and Carolyn F. Donow. "Are We Ready for Ecological Commandments?" *Journal of Environmental Education* 17 (summer 1986): 13-16.

Zimmerman, Michael E., ed. *Environmental Philosophy: From Animal Rights to Radical Ecology.* Englewood Cliffs, NJ: Prentice Hall, 1993.

Zuefle, David Mathew. "Animal Rights Versus Environmental Ethics." *Legacy* 7 (March/April 1996): 31-35.

Index

land, 48
  as community, xv, 55–56, 62
"The Land Ethic" (Leopold), 56
land management, xxii, 55
  practices, 12
Laws of Ecology, 40
learner outcomes, 48
Leopold, Aldo, xiii, xv, xvii, 23, 38–39, 55–56, 62, 93, 94, 105
Levin, Jack, 6
Lewis, Hunter, 70
Lickona, Thomas, 68, 75–76
List, Peter C., 61
literature
  activities involving, 119–121
Loewy, Erich, 77–78

Machlis, Gary, 48–49
Macy, Joanna, 106
Mander, Jerry, 25
masks
  activities involving, 106–107
Maslow, Abraham H., 67
Matthews, Bruce E., 47, 75, 76
McClaren, Milton, 20–21, 50–51, 78, 107
McKibben, Bill, 13
Mead, Margaret, 50
Mencken, H. L., xvii
Merchant, Carolyn, 53
Miller, G. Tyler, Jr., 6, 7, 50
Mills, Stephanie, 58
Momaday, N. Scott, 58, 59
monkey-wrenching, 62
Monroe, Martha C., 80
moral development, 74
moral education, 34, 67, 71
morals, 70
Muir, John, 2, 13, 57
Mumford, Lewis, 57
My First Summer in the Sierra (Muir), 13

Naess, Arne, xiii, 57, 58, 106